The Making
of
Dutch Towns

Printed by George Pulman & Sons

View of Delft by Jan Vermeer (1632–1675)

The Making of Dutch Towns

A Study in Urban Development
from the Tenth to the Seventeenth
Centuries

By

GERALD L. BURKE

M.C., M.SC., F.R.I.C.S., A.M.T.P.I.

Foreword by

Sir William Holford

M.A., B.ARCH., F.R.I.B.A., P.P.T.P.I.
Professor of Town Planning
University of London

LONDON
Cleaver-Hume Press Ltd

CLEAVER-HUME PRESS LTD
31 Wright's Lane, Kensington
London W.8

First Published
1956

Printed in Great Britain by
Western Printing Services Ltd., Bristol

Foreword

by

SIR WILLIAM HOLFORD

ENGLISH writers and sociologists, geographers and town planners, are only just beginning the systematic study of urban societies and the making of towns. This is strange, because at various times the English have been considerable town builders and have embarked on fourteen new ones since the last world war. Moreover, they have been active in promoting social legislation to combat the evils of industrialism and the growth of numbers: they produced in the nineteenth century a great many plans for model villages and garden cities: they have contributed much to formal studies of other aspects of history, economics and law: and they now constitute one of the most urban nations of the globe.

But there is not, as yet, any comprehensive history, in English, of town planning and town building throughout the world. Instead we have a number of studies, of two main kinds, which are providing the basic material for such a history and at the same time are helping to narrow down its very broad and sometimes hazy limits. One kind concerns itself with a special subject within the wider field, such as demography or civic architecture or urban estate management: the other studies the evolution of towns individually or in particular countries or regions.

Mr. Burke's study is of the latter kind, and its subject is the Netherlands up to the end of the seventeenth century. This approximate limit of date, however, by no means limits the contemporary value of his material nor the lessons to be directly drawn from it.

This attractive and fully illustrated book has plenty of academic interest, and for cartographers a special charm; but it has also much practical significance for town planning and local government in Britain at the present time. Holland was a welfare state before us, just as she preceded us in the textile industry, in the money market, and as an international carrier. And in such matters as the control of building development, and the limitation of town growth, her past history is of present interest.

At one time competition between the two countries led directly to war. Now it is more often an incentive towards finding solutions to common problems of peaceful development—problems of population, of assimilating technical change, of congestion of traffic and buildings, and most of all of finding democratic processes by which plans and proposals can be considered, adopted and carried out, perhaps with some hardship but without serious injustice to any section of the community. In this, the most difficult of all the social arts, the Dutch have long experience. Their battle against the sea has been so long and so constant that they are used to sinking lesser differences and to accepting a certain discipline in their environment.

The results, in terms of civic design, have not filled the architectural history books nor caused great excitement in the realm of aesthetic criticism. Perhaps the cult of architectural personality which grew up during the Renaissance put into the background the more solid achievements of the engineers and town builders and administrators in the Low Countries. Yet it is noteworthy that these, having triumphed over appalling difficulties in their own uncompromising terrain, were sent for to the Fen Country and to Denmark, to Poland and Germany and to Russia, and overseas to Batavia and the Cape, where they advised on fortifications, drainage schemes and land reclamation, and undertook the design of canals, parks and urban development plans.

Whatever the cause, Dutch town-building achievements, with the possible exception of Amsterdam, have not been adequately recognized. Mr. Burke's book goes a long way to make good this deficiency. His account of the building, and the subsequent survival and extension, of small towns in Holland is carefully and affectionately done. Nearly a hundred of his own photographs illustrate this book, along with some useful diagrams of town types and layouts, and the reproduction of some attractive and interesting maps, including examples from Jacob van Deventer and Joannes Blaeu. Both in topography and typography the Dutch set a high standard.

This book should be useful to students of social history and geography, municipal engineering and surveying; and it is a real contribution to the town planner's small but growing library. More than that, I hope it will be read by everyone interested in the building of towns and in the formation of urban character, and that means a high proportion of those who live and work in these islands on the other side of the North Sea.

University College, London   WILLIAM HOLFORD
May 1956

Preface

THE past half-century has witnessed an almost world-wide renewal of interest and activity in the art of town building, and this has been accompanied by an increase in published studies concerned with the historical development of towns. The scope of the subject is vast, both in space and in time, and its bibliography is as yet far from adequate. In Europe, the glory that was Greece and the grandeur that was Rome have inspired illuminating works and detailed studies; the informal beauty, humanity in scale and compactness in arrangement of mediaeval towns have claimed the attention of artists and architects, sociologists and planners, and research into the great thirteenth-century programme of new-town building by such scholars as T. F. Tout has encouraged others to follow in his footsteps; the architectural magnificence, bold conception in plan and grand scale in achievement of the Renaissance era have similarly stimulated enthusiastic contributions. But the student of town-planning history, searching for published material in the English language, will encounter many a deficiency even in such well-explored territory as France and Belgium, Germany and Italy; and for other countries such as Scandinavia or the Netherlands he will discover that information is disappointingly sparse.

This book represents an attempt at exploration of ground already well covered by Dutchmen, but by comparatively few others. It gives a brief account of urban and rural evolution in a country which, endowed initially with the poorest of natural resources, stood in constant danger, throughout the ages, of losing most of them to the depredations of the North Sea. There is much to be admired in the results of early Dutch town-planning. There is even more to be admired in the manner in which those results were achieved. The qualities of courage and tenacity, ingenuity and faith displayed in the face of such national disasters as the St. Elizabeth Flood of 1421 or the tragic events of February, 1953, are those of a people with deep and abiding attachment to their homeland who sought from earliest times, and still seek, to extend its area by winning new territory from sea and lake, marsh and bog, instead of casting covetous eyes upon the lands of their neighbours.

London
August 1955
GERALD L. BURKE

7

Acknowledgements

GRATEFUL acknowledgement is made to those who organized and gave lectures for the summer courses "Culture of Cities" and "Civilization and Modern Society" at the University of Leiden in 1947 and 1948, respectively, from which the first ideas for this book were gained; to de Heer Ir S. J. van Emb-den, b.i., for his suggestions regarding bibliography; to de Heer Mr S. J. Fockema Andreae, whose work *Stad en Dorp* in *Duizend Jaar Bouwen in Neder-land* provided such valuable signposts for the author's exploration of the Nether-lands; to the Librarian of the Technische Hoogeschool, Delft, and the staff of the Maps Library, British Museum, for their courteous assistance; to the Directors and staff of the Rijksdienst voor het Nationale Plan and the Nederlands Insti-tuut voor Volkshuisvesting en Stedebouw, for information concerning land reclamation; to the Central Research Fund Committee of the University of London for the grant awarded in respect of the author's dissertation for the degree of M.Sc. in Estate Management, from which the present work is derived; and to the Trustees of the British Museum for permission to reproduce the town maps.

The author is much indebted to his brother, Edmund V. Burke, B.A., and Jhr. Ir E. A. L. Gevaerts, m.i., who read the draft and made most helpful com-ments; to Mr. C. C. Brearley, who drew the geographical maps and diagrams; to Professors Sir William Holford and W. G. East, for criticisms and suggestions made when they examined the dissertation, and especially to the former for kindly consenting to write a Foreword. He is particularly grateful to de Heer Mr A. L. W. van Heel for seeking and verifying information on his behalf and, finally, to his wife for her patient and invaluable co-operation in translation of the many Dutch works to which reference had to be made.

Contents

List of Illustrations

CONTEMPORARY VIEWS

TOWN PLANS

Concerning Sources of Contemporary Town Plans, see Appendix

LIST OF ILLUSTRATIONS

PHOTOGRAPHS

LINE MAPS AND PLANS

Map 2 is taken from *Dredge, Drain, Reclaim* by Dr. J. van Veen; the others are based upon those shown in the *Historische School Atlas* of H. Hettema, Jnr.

To men of other minds my fancy flies,
Embosom'd in the deep where Holland lies.
Methinks her patient sons before me stand,
Where the broad ocean leans against the land,
And, sedulous to stop the coming tide,
Lift the tall rampire's artificial pride.
Onward, methinks, and diligently slow,
The firm-connected bulwark seems to grow;
Spreads its long arms amidst the watery roar,
Scoops out an empire, and usurps the shore:
While the pent ocean rising o'er the pile,
Sees an amphibious world beneath him smile;
The slow canal, the yellow-blossom'd vale,
The willow-tufted bank, the gliding sail,
The crowded mart, the cultivated plain,—
A new creation rescued from his reign.

OLIVER GOLDSMITH, *The Traveller*

1. *Modern Netherlands showing location of towns referred to in text*

CHAPTER I

Background to Development Until 1400

THE LAND

DURING the last phase of the Ice Age, the Netherlands formed part of a continental land mass of much greater area than modern Europe. The prehistoric continental coastline extended, at times, as far as Scotland and Jutland; Britain was linked by land with France; and the Thames and the Humber were tributaries of the Rhine. As the climate grew milder, and melting ice released immense quantities of water, the sea level rose and the plains between Britain and Denmark and much of the western part of the Netherlands became submerged. About 5000 B.C. the waters of the Atlantic forced their way past what are now the cliffs of Dover to rejoin the North Sea; and in doing so they scoured sand from the southern shallows and swept it up to form a continuous bank, upon which the prevailing south and west winds built the dunes that constitute approximately the modern coastline of the Netherlands. Behind the dunes a large lagoon came into being into which the Rhine and the Meuse, now forced to seek new outlets to the sea, deposited their loads of silt and gradually built up a wide belt of alluvial plain between the higher ground to the north and south. Thus the Netherlands began to assume something like their present shape, although they were to undergo many geographical changes, some of great violence, before the dividing line between land and sea attained a measure of stability. The ingenuity and persistence of human effort was also to play a vital part in preserving the balance between the elements—a balance which, even today, is somewhat precarious.

By the first century A.D. the coastal dunes had consolidated into a fairly firm, though not always effective, barrier against the sea. Behind them had formed belts of *geestgrond*, a mixture of clay, peat and archaic sand dunes, which ran roughly parallel with the coastline and occasionally penetrated in tongues into a wide, marshy area studded with lakes that remained from the lagoon. Further eastwards, a few hundred feet above sea level, lay sandy heaths and high fens. The central river plain formed by the Rhine, Lek, Waal and Meuse, together with a long and almost continuous belt of waterlogged flats along the

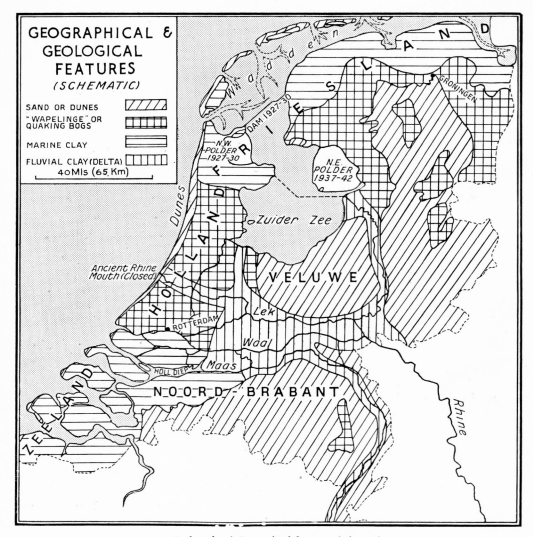

GEOGRAPHICAL &
GEOLOGICAL
FEATURES
(SCHEMATIC)

SAND OR DUNES

"WAPELINGE" OR
QUAKING BOGS

MARINE CLAY

FLUVIAL CLAY (DELTA)

40 Mls (65 Km)

2. Geological and Geographical formation (schematic)

eastern boundary, isolated the greater part of the country from the remainder of
Europe. Some indication of these physical features is given in the map (*2*). The
land was constantly exposed to the violence of North Sea gales and constantly
threatened by inundation from without and within: the sea worried ceaselessly at
the coast-line and sometimes penetrated parts of it; the great rivers and lakes were
always liable to flood the surrounding countryside and frequently did so.

The dunes, which were formed in a double row, did not remain on fixed alignments throughout the centuries but were shifted intermittently by strong currents or high winds. Parts of the outer chain were formerly inhabited; the Romans built their fortress of Brittenburg to command the point where the Rhine at one time entered the sea, but it has long been destroyed following an eastward move of the dunes and its remains can occasionally be seen far out at very low tide. The map (3) shows a fairly continuous line of dunes and a Flevo Lacus (Zuider Zee) of moderate size. By the end of the fifth century a great change began to take place in the geography of the country. The land had been consolidating and its general level was sinking very slowly; and a succession of storms of unusual violence battered the shores so heavily that the northern and southern dunes could no longer withstand the pressure. In the north the deep inlet of the Wadden was made and the extent of the Zuider Zee greatly increased; in the south the land was broken up into the many islands of the Zeeland archipelago and the wide estuary of the Scheldt came into being (see map 5).

The peat-bog areas of Friesland and Groningen, and to a lesser extent those of Zeeland, afforded good grazing behind the dunes but permanent and safe habitation for men and cattle could only be secured by constructing mounds of mud, spadeful by spadeful, ramming and consolidating, and building huts on top of them. These mounds, called *terpen* or *wierden*, varied in area from five to forty acres and were originally made of sufficient height to protect their occupants against the normal rise of the tide. In the first century some twelve hundred terps are said to have existed in the country.[1] The elder Pliny, who served with the Roman legions about the year A.D. 50, gave a first-hand account of the terps and their inhabitants; in discussing the life led by people in countries devoid of trees and shrubs he wrote as follows:

"We have indeed stated that in the east, on the shores of the ocean, a number of races are in this necessitious condition; but so also are the races of people called the Greater and the Lesser Chauci, whom we have seen in the north. There twice in each period of a day and a night the ocean with its vast tide sweeps in a flood over a measureless expanse, covering up Nature's age-long controversy and the region disputed as belonging whether to the land or to the sea. There this miserable race occupy elevated patches of ground or platforms built up by hand above the level of the highest tide experienced, living in huts erected on the sites so chosen, and resembling sailors in ships when the water covers the surrounding land, but shipwrecked people when the tide has retired, and round their huts they catch the fish escaping with the receding tide. It does not fall to them to keep herds and live on milk like the neighbouring tribes, nor even to have to fight with wild animals, as all woodland growth is banished far away. They twine ropes of sedge and rushes from the marshes for the purpose of setting nets to catch the fish, and they scoop up mud in their hands and dry it more by the wind than by sunshine, and with turves as fuel warm their food and so their own bodies, frozen by the north wind. Their only drink is supplied by storing rain water in tanks in the forecourts of their homes. And these are the people that if they are nowadays vanquished by the Roman nation say that they are reduced to slavery!"[2]

Pliny apparently did not see the terp-dwellers further inland who did keep cattle. The terps were in course of time increased in height and extent by the accumulated debris of settlement until they were large enough to accommodate villages and towns; the capital of Friesland, Leeuwarden, had its origin in a cluster of them.

The western lowlands, a dreary expanse of swamp, bog (*wapelinge*) and lake with here and there a little grazing for cattle, provided the most meagre of livings for only a few groups of marshmen. Scarcely any settlement or cultivation took place there until the eleventh century, when attempts were made to stem the widespread seasonal floods by building dikes to hold rivers in their courses and to contain the larger lakes. This work was later rewarded with great success, as will be noted in Chapter VI, but many grave setbacks were experienced over the centuries. The greatest on record was the appalling Flood of St. Elizabeth in 1421, in which failure of the Meuse dikes resulted in the formation of the Hollandse Diep (south of Dordrecht) and the marshy wilderness of the Biesbos; in this disaster thousands of acres were engulfed and seventy-two villages and some ten thousand people disappeared. About this time, also, the Zuider Zee reached its maximum extent and the wide basin of the Dollard was formed east of Groningen (compare maps 5 and 6).

It was an irony of fate that the only parts of the Netherlands high enough to permit of safe and permanent habitation in early centuries were insufficiently fertile to support a population. The area south-east of the Zuider Zee, known as the Veluwe which means "bad soil", and other districts in the eastern and southern provinces have sterile soil and poor natural drainage. Although they give evidence of occupation by prehistoric man, settlement there during historical times has always been sparse and the scarcity of towns in these regions is as noticeable on maps of today as of centuries ago.

18

THE PEOPLE

The first-century inhabitants of the Netherlands were of Germanic and Celtic origin. The lands north of the Rhine were peopled chiefly by primitive Germanic tribes who had migrated westwards during previous centuries in search of better grazing land. They found it in the present provinces of Friesland and Groningen but had to build terps to protect themselves and their cattle against annual floods. A more advanced Germanic tribe, the Batavi, occupied the so-called "Isle of the Batavi", the fertile lands between the Rhine and the Meuse. They were essentially a fighting people and acted as mercenaries in the Roman armies; many of them saw service in Britain and elsewhere in Europe. Under their leader Civilis, and in concert with other tribes, they were able to inflict a major defeat on the Roman armies during an uprising about the year A.D. 70 but retaliation by the Imperial forces a few years later resulted in their virtual loss of entity as a people. South of the Rhine Celtic warrior tribes had settled during the last two centuries B.C. on both sides of the Meuse as far north as Nijmegen and also in eastern Brabant. Their practice of La Tène art connotes an advanced cultural state which subsequent centuries of contact with their traditional enemies, the Romans, served to maintain and improve.

The latest large-scale movement of Germanic tribes into Friesland took place about the beginning of the fifth century, and archaeological evidence suggests that the immigrants came from the coastal districts of Hanover and Schleswig. Since the end of the fifth century, although individual immigration still took place and small groups of refugees and settlers continued to add new elements to the population, it is considered that the racial composition of the people has not been greatly altered.[3]

During the first ten centuries of our era, the people were subjected to a pattern of events similar to that experienced by others of Western Europe. Four centuries of contact with the Roman Empire were succeeded by three centuries of anarchy and barbarism; a breathing space of less than a century under a strong Frankish monarchy ended abruptly in a ferocious Danish domination; and this was followed by the gradual emergence of feudalism. To the ravages of invading man were added the violence and destruction of an invading sea. The development of the country in such circumstances must have been a heartbreaking and backbreaking task. The people who accomplished it, inured by generations of adversity, arose in the Middle Ages as toughened, independent and freedom-loving individuals. Their energy, ability and strength of character enabled them

19

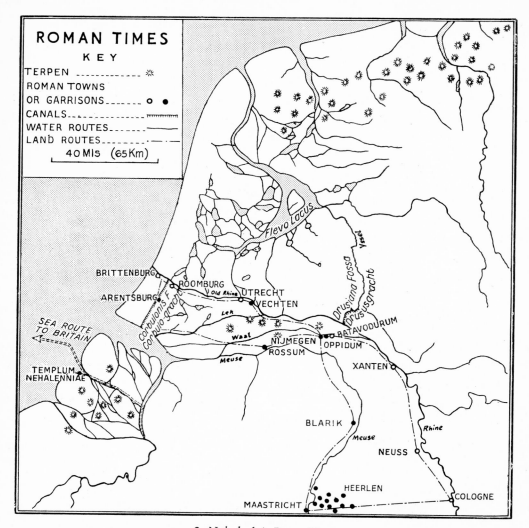

3. *Netherlands in Roman Times*

to compete successfully with the rest of Europe and, in the seventeenth century, to dominate the world's trade.

ROMAN OCCUPATION

The limit in Northern Europe of the Roman Empire, even at its greatest extent during the third century A.D., was the main stream of the Rhine from Cologne and its continuation via Utrecht to the fortress of Brittenburg (map *3*). The area

20

north of this line was seldom penetrated by the Roman soldier or trader; for them these uninviting lands remained virtually *terra incognita*. To the south, however, the country was of strategic importance, and during the first large-scale occupation under the general Drusus Nero some fifty fortresses were built along the course of the Rhine. The legions used the "Island of the Batavi" as their main base for controlling the area and for assembling armies in preparation for the conquest of German territory as far as the Elbe.

The Romans' chief interest in the country lay in its navigable waterways, which provided transport routes for both troops and merchandise. The Rhine at that time had three main branches: the most northerly, the Old Rhine, which flowed via Utrecht to Brittenburg, was not uniformly navigable but petered out into marshland near Roomburg; the two navigable branches were the Lek and the Waal. Drusus did much to improve the system of waterways and had dikes constructed at vulnerable points to prevent flooding. He made a remarkably intrepid voyage into the unknown when, in 9 B.C., he sailed from the Rhine to the Flevo Lacus. Some five years later he constructed an important link between the Rhine and the Ijssel to afford direct contact with the Flevo Lacus. Dannett, translating Guicciardini in 1593, describes the achievement in these words:

"Drusus Nero, seeing no great distance to be between this right branch of the Rhine (near Arnhem) and the river Ijssel . . . cutte a large Fosse neere to Arnhem, all the waie between Arnhem and Doesburg, into which he received part of the water of this right branch of the Rhine, the which conveying by this Fosse to Doesburg, he there joyned with the river Ijssel to convey the easier the Roman army out of the Rhine into the Septentrionell Sea. This Fosse being joyned with the Ijssel at Campen entereth into the gulf of Zuider Zee."[1]

Later, about A.D. 45, the general Corbulo had a canal of some twenty-three miles length dug between the Old Rhine near Roomburg and the mouth of the Meuse which provided a more efficient route from Brittenburg and Roomburg and the river ports of Utrecht and Vechten to the North Sea.

The Romans formulated no comprehensive road system for the Netherlands. A few routes were constructed alongside rivers to connect fortresses, and Drusus built a highway beside the Rhine, but only one major road came anywhere near the country. This was the great highway from Cologne to Boulogne which crossed the Meuse at Maastricht and continued through the then metropolis of Greater Netherlands, the town of Tongeren in Belgium. In one respect this highway had a similar function to that of the Fosse Way in Britain: it fixed the dividing line between the regions which had become Romanized and those less peacefully occupied. It continued to mark the furthest extent of Germanic influence for many centuries to come.

The "villa" system of agricultural settlement was well established in the lands bordering this highway but little evidence of such colonization has been found much further north. The forbidding, marshy lands held out no promise of economic farming and the Imperial granaries could be more easily stocked from other sources. Apart, therefore, from a few river ports, Maastricht on the Meuse, Nijmegen on the Waal and Utrecht and Vechten on the Old Rhine, the first stages in the advancement of the Netherlands saw little benefit from a civilization that had bestowed such great assets upon other countries.

ROMAN AFTERMATH

The three centuries which followed the evacuation of the Legions were for the southern part of these lands, as for most areas of Romanized Europe, times of violence and disintegration. Such progress and urban civilization as had been achieved during the four centuries of Pax Romana was demolished in the course of a few decades by Germanic hordes of many tribes. The conditions under which urban civilization is tenable, namely the production or importation of food, a well-ordered system of trading, the maintenance of protection, law and order, and a central political direction, did not prevail again in the Netherlands until the rise of the Carolingian Empire.

Nevertheless the Frisian settlers north of the Rhine, left comparatively undisturbed by the invaders who preferred to plunder richer districts in Gaul, were beginning to open up a trading relationship destined to prove of vital significance to the Netherlands of the Middle Ages. The Romans, with their notorious dislike of long sea voyages, had largely neglected the possibilities of trade with the economically backward countries bordering the eastern shores of the North Sea and the Baltic; the Frisians, however, gradually developed commercial contacts with these distant regions, and their port of Dorestad (map 5) admirably situated at the confluence of the Old Rhine and the Lek, grew to prosperity as a result of such pioneering trade, as well as by that which passed through it from the great emporium of Cologne.

The eighth century saw a renewal of effort in another important aspect of national development. Experience of terp building had led to experiments in dike building; and the Frisians, taking up the task abandoned after the Roman evacuation, started to build river dikes to protect land liable to seasonal flooding. They also dammed and reclaimed tidal marshes which, during calm periods, had gradually risen above the level of high tide. New land was thus brought into use for cultivation and pasture but to win and maintain it was a long and at times hazardous process. Ancient Frisian law gives powerful expression to the determination never to yield such hard-won land, with these words: "With five weapons shall we keep our land, with sword and shield, with spade and fork and with the spear, out with the ebb, up with the flood, to fight day and night against the North King (the sea) and against the wild Viking, that all Frisians may be free, the born and the unborn, so long as the wind from the clouds shall blow and the world shall stand."[5]

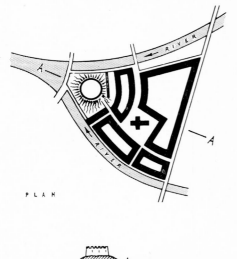

PLAN

SECTION A-A

4. *Burcht Town: Leiden*

CAROLINGIAN INFLUENCE

Towards the end of the eighth century the Netherlands became part of the empire of Charles the Great, and the country was divided into large estates administered by his bishops and nobles. Christianity had made considerable headway following the labours of two Anglo-Saxon missionaries St. Willibrord, the "apostle of the Frisians" and first Bishop of Utrecht who died in 739, and his successor St. Boniface who was martyred at Dokkum in 755. Its continued progress tended to unite the people and encouraged them to live together in larger communities than before. Social and political institutions gradually evolved; communities became more closely organized and had to pay taxes and render military service.

Urban settlement during the eighth and ninth centuries sometimes had as its focus the burcht, a rounded, man-made hill some 200 feet in diameter and 50 feet or more in height above the surrounding countryside, enclosed at the summit at first by a palisade and later by a brick wall (6). This provided a place of comparative safety to which the people could retire in the event of attack. Middelburg, Oostburg, Den Burg, Doesburg, Breda and Leiden are among the towns which developed from such a nucleus, although the last-named is the only one in which the burcht itself survives.

Settlements of this kind began to emerge as markets and administrative centres.

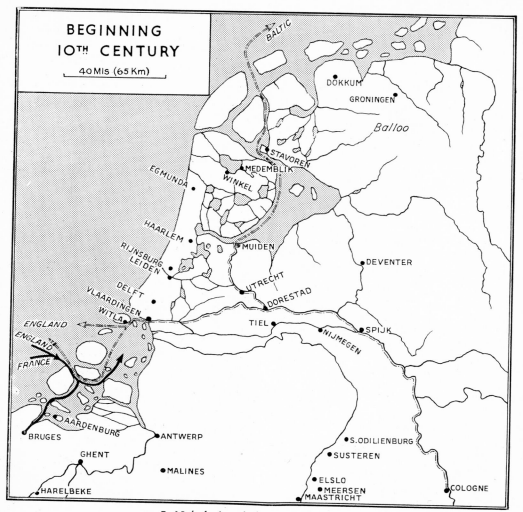

5. Netherlands at the beginning of tenth century

Their inhabitants, according to Blok,[6] included wool-weavers and furriers, leatherworkers and smiths, butchers and bakers, and innkeepers who catered for the needs of itinerant traders. Such early towns were lacking in what Pirenne considered to be the two fundamental attributes of cities of the Middle Ages: they had no middle-class population and no local representative government; they were strongholds for retainers rather than balanced communities with laws and institutions of their own.[7] Motley paints a somewhat gloomy picture of

24

the ninth-century common people: "It was a miserable people with personal but no civic rights whatever. Their condition, although better than servitude, was almost desperate. They were taxed beyond their ability, while priest and noble were exempt. There was no redress against the lawless violence to which they were perpetually exposed. In the manorial courts the criminal sat in judgment upon his victim. The functions of highwayman and magistrate were combined in one individual."[3] He goes on to say, however, that by degrees the people organized themselves into guilds, aided by local lords who were anxious to increase their own importance, and eventually were granted charters which *inter alia* guaranteed government by law instead of by arbitrary violence.

The only towns of any size and importance in this period were Nijmegen, which was popular with the Emperor as a seat of government—the remains of his palace are still preserved there—the river port of Dorestad already referred to, and the trading and religious centres of Utrecht and Maastricht.

THE VIKING INVASIONS

The death of Charles the Great in 814 marked the beginning of disintegration within the vast empire that he had held together with such success. Its division, by the Treaty of Verdun, 843, into three Kingdoms, of the West Franks, the East Franks and Lotharingia, left the last-named—the Middle Kingdom—as a long buffer state stretching from the North Sea to the Mediterranean. Politically as well as geographically an entirely unrealistic and impracticable unit of government, its speedy fragmentation into petty states was a logical outcome.

The remainder of the ninth century was, for the northernmost part of this kingdom, a period of lawlessness and wretchedness. From 834 the Netherlands suffered brutal and reiterated attacks at the hands of Viking invaders whose ships, using the trade routes prospected by the Romans and developed by the Frisians, penetrated as far as Utrecht and Dorestad. They indulged in systematic and persistent pillaging, annihilating villages and hamlets, monasteries and nunneries, and slaughtering their inhabitants. Devastation was so thorough in some places that the entire local population disappeared. By 850 the greater part of Holland and Friesland was under Norse domination. The port of Dorestad, utterly destroyed in 863, was never rebuilt.

Despite this barbaric setback the civilizing influence of Christianity gradually prevailed over the years, and by the turn of the tenth century the comparative peace and order of feudalism had become established. The country was divided into a tangle of fiefs whose rulers owed allegiance, if in most cases only nominal,

25

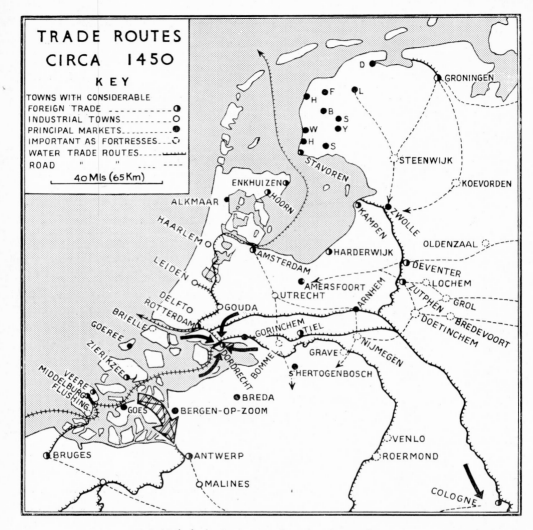

6. Netherlands, circa 1450: trade routes and principal towns

to the Holy Roman Emperor. The weak successors to Charles the Great, unable to protect their people against Viking onslaughts, were equally incapable of enforcing a strong feudal system. Bishops, dukes and counts were able, by virtue of the situation of their fiefs in borderland positions between the developing Kingdom of France and the Germanic states, to secure for themselves an increasing measure of independence.

26

THE MIDDLE AGES

By the middle of the twelfth century the country for the most part enjoyed a fairly stable, feudal government. North of the central river plain the political grouping was in the four states of Holland, Friesland, Utrecht and Gelderland; to the west lay the state of Zeeland and in the south the duchy of Brabant was paramount. Within these states many minor hereditary rulers exercised petty rights.

It is of interest to observe that the social inequalities of feudalism, with its powerful superiors and obedient serfs, were less in evidence in the Netherlands than elsewhere in Europe. Several recorded instances of would-be despots receiving rough treatment at the hands of unyielding subjects show that the common man there had already achieved a considerable degree of independence. This was in part attributable to the fact that the great work of building sea and river dikes was making rapid progress and a constant demand for experienced labour existed in many parts of the country. Thus freedom of movement from one region to another provided a means of escape from the narrow confines of normal feudal society. Moreover this task, while demanding the services of specialists in diking and reclamation, called equally for communal local effort in towns and villages. The threat of inundation was a threat to a community: only a community could hold a dike fast against a flood; only a community could reclaim land for agriculture; only a series of communities could engage in a task of such magnitude as diking the Zuider Zee. Co-operative work of this kind, directed by local dikemasters with little interference from the feudal lord, inculcated in the people a sense of proprietorship: their labours were performed not so much to benefit a remote and unknown landlord as to defeat a common and ever-present enemy, the sea; their efforts were rewarded with new land and, as is universal with peasants, they held on to it obstinately and sought always to gain more. The normal mediaeval community was bound together by the town wall: the Dutch mediaeval community had an even closer tie in the dike. This unity of interest and purpose led to self-reliance in town and village life and, in increasing measure, to active participation in local government.

ECONOMIC DEVELOPMENT

The Netherlands occupied a central position in the closely populated parts of Europe in the Middle Ages. Two very important trade routes intersected the country, one from the Baltic via the Zuider Zee to Flanders and the other from the German hinterland via the Rhine to England (map 6). In addition, an elaborate system of inland waterways afforded easy and cheap means of transport within the country itself. Thus commercial towns began to develop: Deventer, Kampen and Stavoren were key points for twelfth-century Baltic trade, whilst Dordrecht and Tiel (which succeeded Dorestad) were among the larger centres that thrived on the east-west commerce as well. Although the bulk of traffic throughout the Middle Ages was waterborne, several towns grew to importance as road traffic junctions (Amersfoort, Coeworden, Groningen), as links in the road system (Haarlem and Alkmaar in the *geestgrond*), at points where road traffic changed to water traffic or river to sea traffic (Arnhem, Harderwijk, Rotterdam), or at ferries and fords (Utrecht, Nijmegen, Zwolle). Early twelfth-century toll lists, such as those of Coblenz,[9] give an idea of the principal commodities dealt with: from the Rhine came salmon and eels, wax and wines; from coastal areas herrings and salt; from the Baltic and North Sea countries timber and grain; from Friesland cattle, butter and cheese. Further revenue was derived from leather and linen goods, swords, falcons and slaves. A country so meagrely endowed by nature with raw materials had to depend upon its skill in the role of entrepreneur. Wool was imported and cloth exported; grain was imported and beer exported. The leading home industries were fishing, salt refining and dairying. Of these the first two became of outstanding importance following the discovery by William Beukels of Zeeland in 1384 that herrings could be preserved for a considerable time by salting in barrels. The volume of the export trade was, in consequence, enormously increased and great wealth accrued to the country: "Amsterdam was built on herring bones".

TOWN FOUNDATION

Stable government and material prosperity led to the foundation of many towns; in fact, as Tout[10] wrote of this period in Europe as a whole, "the conscious creation of towns on a large scale had become both a political and an economic necessity; with the fever for founding new towns that marked the twelfth and thirteenth centuries the golden age of mediaeval town planning set in".

It will be as well to notice at this point that the word "town" or "city" has a special significance in the Netherlands. Blok, who discusses the matter at length,[11] considers the three claims to the title to lie in the possession of a charter, a market and a wall, and that the charter or statute granted by the sovereign, or by a local lord with or without the sovereign's approval, is the most important. Other authorities support this view, and Brugmans[12] explains that the privileges awarded in the charter, which is in the nature of a treaty between the townspeople and their feudal lord, are not sharply defined but include a large measure of independence for the citizens from the rule of the emperor or local noble, and independence in jurisdiction, finance and military service. Charters are useful in the study of the history of Dutch towns, for they fix the date when an existing settlement was elevated to town status, or the date of foundation of a new town. Peters[13] gives lists of towns which had received their municipal rights before the thirteenth century (he cites twelve), during the thirteenth century (sixty-two), during the fourteenth century (sixty-seven), during the fifteenth century (forty-four) and the sixteenth century (two: the new towns of Willemstad and Klundert). Among them are several which have since vanished as a result of destruction by the sea.

Although the power of town foundation in the early Middle Ages vested theoretically in the Emperor, it had by delegation or otherwise passed into the hands of feudal rulers. But no ruler was ever able to found a town merely by granting a charter: the town found its *raison d'être* and its growth primarily in production and trade. Thus the charter was an official acknowledgement of what had, in fact, taken place: it did not create a town but rather sanctioned and promoted development. Local rulers often showed considerable insight in this respect, and naturally used their official power to strengthen their own position. They chose sites for towns which had strategic importance, for example at ferries or toll points, and did all they could to attract traffic to them; they encouraged development where it best suited their policy and, wherever the opportunity arose, they set up towns in rivalry with those of neighbouring rulers.

Nijmegen and Arnhem provide an example of the last-named practice. The former, as already noticed, was an ancient settlement enjoying a very favourable situation at the point of change between water and overland traffic routes and commanding the main trade artery from the eastern hinterland to the delta between the Rhine and the Meuse. The Count of Gelderland, who controlled the area immediately north of the city, endeavoured to divert Nijmegen's trade by establishing Arnhem on the Lek, some ten miles away. It occupied the site of a former market village and was developed in accordance with a detailed plan as a new and great city. Similarly Zutphen was fostered and enlarged during the thirteenth century as a rival to the old Hanseatic port of Deventer which, until then, had a virtual monopoly of the Ijssel traffic. In neither case was the trade entirely captured by the new foundation, but shared. Even in modern times a certain spirit of rivalry still persists between each pair.

INFLUENCE OF MONASTERIES

Mumford asserts[14] that the rise of early mediaeval towns was due more to the influence of monasteries during the tenth century than to the great revival of trade in the eleventh century. As far as the Netherlands are concerned, however, their influence as town builders seems to have been only an indirect one. Monks and missionaries had been active in the country from the seventh century onwards, and during the twelfth century Cistercians, Augustinians and Benedictines laboured vigorously in rural areas, where they added to their spiritual and cultural achievements the reclamation of much land and improvement in agricultural methods. Their influence in towns before the twelfth century, however, seems to have been but slight; abbeys prominent in such towns as Middelburg, Utrecht Deventer, Delft and Haarlem were all of twelfth-century date. The great orders remained mostly in the countryside and only the mendicant friars, Dominicans and Franciscans, worked in the towns and later built their small chapels and convents, *gasthuisen* (hospitals) and *hofjes* (almshouses) along the streets. Verheijen[15] adduces no instance in which towns grew up around monasteries; indeed it seems that town councils did their best to keep these buildings outside town limits. Nor does Ganshoff[16] in his detailed anaylsis of the origins of mediaeval towns point to any specific case of monasteries founding towns in the Netherlands. It can be concluded, therefore, that monastic orders assisted the development of towns by founding schools and providing for the sick and the poor, but that the control they exercised over urban affairs was less powerful than elsewhere in Europe.

*   *   *   *   *   *

The first ten centuries of its history presaged for the Netherlands no rapid rise to a leading position among the countries of Europe. A remote and forbidding outpost of the Roman Empire, peculiarly ill-endowed with natural resources, its low-lying regions a prey to violent seas and fierce gales and its higher regions for the most part sandy wastes, it offered no great attraction for settlement. The Romans had shown little interest in anything but its waterways, nor did the Franks have much to contribute towards its promotion as a civilized land. It was not until the Baltic trade route had been opened up by the early Frisians, and grim advertisement given to it by invading Vikings, that the country's favourable commercial situation began to be realized. By the twelfth century the "Ijssel towns", Deventer, Zwolle and Kampen, had acquired a large share of the Hanseatic trade. By the end of the following century increased activity along the Rhine route and in overseas trade had brought the promise of great prosperity to Holland and Zeeland. The country thus found itself at mediaeval Europe's commercial crossroads and its merchants were quick to take advantage of the fact. Towns developed and expanded upon sites which, physically, were most inappropriate for the purpose; but no better could be found in the locations where trade required them to be. Dutch towns were comparative late-comers in Europe, but once established their rise was rapid and their prosperity enduring.

REFERENCES

1. VAN VEEN, J., *Dredge, Drain, Reclaim*, 1948, p. 21.
2. PLINY, *Naturalis Historia*, Books XVI–XVII, trans. H. Rackham.
3. VLEKKE, B. H. M., *Evolution of the Dutch Nation*, 1951, p. 17.
4. GUICCIARDINI, L., *Description of the Low Countreys . . .*, trans. G. Dannett, London, 1593, p. 5.
5. VAN VEEN, J., *op. cit.*, p. 21.
6. BLOK, P. J., *History of the Dutch People*, 1898–1912, Vol. I, p. 6.
7. PIRENNE, H., *Mediaeval Cities*, 1925, p. 57.
8. MOTLEY, J. L., *The Rise of the Dutch Republic*, 1864, Vol. I, p. 34.
9. BLOK, P. J., *op. cit.*, Vol. I, pp. 112–13.
10. TOUT, T. F., *Mediaeval Town Planning*, 1934, p. 7.
11. BLOK, P. J., *op. cit.*, Vol. I, p. 217.
12. BRUGMANS, H., *Staatkundig en Maatschappelijk Leven der Nederlandsche Steden*, 1909, p. 7.
13. PETERS, C. H., *De Nederlandsche Stedenbouw*, 1909, Vol. II, pp. 441–3.
14. MUMFORD, L., *The Culture of Cities*, 1940, p. 17.
15. VERHEIJEN, J., *Middeleeuwsche Nederlandsche Kloosters*, 1947.
16. GANSHOFF, E. L., *Etude sur le Développement des Villes entre Loire et Rhin au Moyen Age*, 1943.

CHAPTER II

Mediaeval Town Foundation
and Development: I

Dike and Dike-and-Dam Towns, Seaports

ORIGINS OF TOWNS

THE point has often been made by town-planning historians that some towns have grown gradually from some small nucleus whilst others were developed *ab initio* in accordance with a predetermined pattern. There are far more in the first group, the "chance-grown" towns, than in the latter, the "planned" towns.

The factors which have determined the location, size and prosperity of the world's towns have been, in the main, the physical features of the surface—the nature of the soil and sub-soil, the course and depth of a river and its fordable points, the configuration of the valleys and of the seashore, the wealth of mineral deposits at a workable depth, or perhaps even the presence of a spring of medicinal value. But location was often influenced by factors other than physical: some towns owed their existence to the siting of a castle or a monastery; some were planned as adjuncts to a ruler's residence, some as components of a regional defence pattern; some were founded for political reasons, others for administrative convenience. Some which had their origin in a particular set of circumstances continued to exist in the face of quite different circumstances, their function changing with developments in trade, industry or methods of transport; others declined when the reason for which they were founded ceased to be of significance.

The origin of most of the world's towns can be traced back to some early nucleus of a few houses or huts having as its *raison d'être* one or more of the above factors. The nucleus gradually expanded in a fortuitous manner, buildings being added as the site dictated but without plan. Even the most prolific planners of new towns, the Romans, generally chose sites which had previously been occupied, possibly centuries before, by Neolithic settlers and their various successors, Phoenicians, Greeks, Celts or Belgae; for the reasons which made such

32

sites suitable for settlement in the first place still obtained in Roman times and, in many cases, still obtain today. If these pre-Roman settlements had some degree of order in their layout as, for example, those of Hellenistic Greece, the Roman town usually took the form of a regularization and an extension of its predecessor and the original pattern was largely preserved. Nevertheless many new towns were founded on virgin sites, as the colonies of Alexander the Great or of Rome; and some hundreds were planned and built during the twelfth and thirteenth centuries. Prominent among these last were the military towns known as *bastides* or *villeneuves* or *nieuwesteden*.

Of Netherlands towns it may be said that a higher proportion than elsewhere in Europe belong to the "planned" group than to the "chance-grown"; and that even of those in the latter group the kernel of settlement existing before the tenth century was usually so small as to be of little influence upon later development as a town. Exceptions can be made to this generalization, but evidence in support of it can be adduced from study of the geography of settlement.

It was shown earlier that the western regions of the Netherlands have always been in a state of instability—now increasing as a result of reclamation of sea, lake, river or marsh, now decreasing as a result of inundation. A vital preliminary to town foundation in such circumstances was the choice of a site which had safety and stability. The earliest settlement therefore took place on such ground above high-tide level as was available: on islands, as Dordrecht and Middelburg, on the natural eminence that often occurs at the confluence of rivers, as Nijmegen and Dorestad, on the geestgrond, as Haarlem or Alkmaar, on naturally high ground, as Amersfoort and Utrecht, or on raised ground, as the dikes or the terps of Friesland, Groningen and, to a lesser extent, Zeeland. Frequently, however, particularly in the western lowlands, the site had to be drained, consolidated and raised above the level of the surrounding countryside before any building could be undertaken, and large buildings had to be supported on deep-driven piles (the town hall, now royal palace, of Amsterdam rests on 13,659 piles, and the pile-drivers are even now busy with the rebuilding of Rotterdam). The development of towns in such circumstances could not, therefore, as often elsewhere in Europe, be casual or fortuitous: it had to proceed as a conscious, regulated expansion in accordance with a detailed plan.

It is noticeable, therefore, that whilst the oldest parts of Dutch towns built upon naturally high ground may present a somewhat haphazard picture, with street lines and scenes reminiscent of mediaeval towns in other countries, those on ground less firm and more vulnerable to flooding bear every sign of premeditated layout and strict control. The "scattered city" could never be typical of the Netherlands; in country where it is impossible to erect an important building except on a site specially prepared for it, sporadic growth is out of the question.

BUILDING MATERIALS

Permanent materials for house building were employed at a rather earlier date in the Netherlands than elsewhere in Europe. Very little local stone was available; the small quantities that could with difficulty be extracted from the Rhine or the Meuse, or that occurred in Twente or South Limburg, were used mostly for church building. Bricks had been introduced by the Romans and were certainly used in the reconstruction of the wall enclosing the Burcht at Leiden about the year 1300, but when they became adopted as the normal building material is a matter for speculation. The authorities[1] are in agreement that brick was in general use by the middle of the thirteenth century for churches, town halls and the houses of wealthy citizens, but the contemporary small man's dwelling was the low, thatched wooden house later provided with a brick façade. Such buildings were a prey to disastrous town fires, in which it was not uncommon for half or three-quarters of the built-up area to be destroyed on a single occasion. Although few of the buildings existing in Dutch mediaeval towns today can be of much earlier date than 1500, the comparative stability of urban life in the fifteenth and sixteenth centuries makes it not an unreasonable assumption that town layouts as portrayed on sixteenth-century maps were much the same on the ground two or three centuries previously.

TOWN LAYOUTS

Mediaeval towns in the Netherlands display a remarkable variety in their layout, attributable to a similar variety in the sites upon which they developed. Natural high ground, man-made high ground, geestgrond or reclaimed ground all called for different treatment which yielded, as will be seen, different characteristic town patterns.

It was remarked earlier that the powerful magnet of trade attracted urban development to sites which, physically, were singularly unattractive for the purpose; and also that diking of rivers and construction of canals protected on either side by dikes were among the earliest works carried out to improve communications for local and foreign trade. The dikes themselves were normally

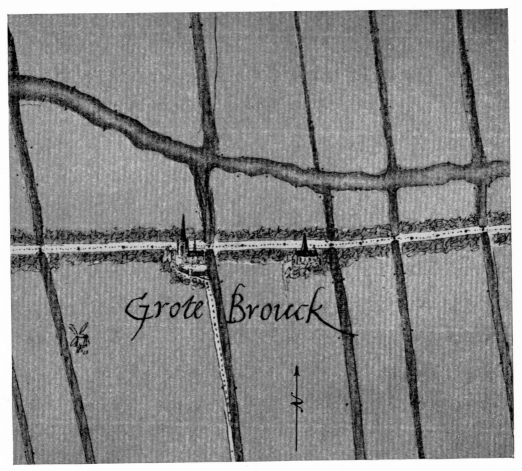

7. *Grootebroek, circa 1580 (Jacob van Deventer)*

made of sufficient width to allow for a road to run along the top and for buildings to be erected upon the berms, and they also afforded protection against flooding to any extension of building which might be required on the lower ground behind them. It is to be expected, therefore, that many towns in low-lying areas were built upon dikes, and that parts of several towns founded alongside important trade waterways show the characteristic dike-town formation; examples are Leiden, which grew upon the dikes of the "Old" and "New" Rhines, Rotter-dam along the Rotte, Amsterdam along the Amstel and Gouda along the Gouwe.

DIKE TOWNS

The layout of the dike town is most clearly seen in numerous small settle⁄ments in lowland areas, and its princi⁄pal feature is what has come to be known in the twentieth century as "rib⁄bon development". That this feature is no special achievement of modern times is evident from the plan (7) of the four⁄teenth⁄century town of Grootebroek, North Holland, drawn by Jacob van Deventer about 1560. A similarly striking example in the same region is Broek⁄op⁄Langedijk. Settlements of this kind usually originated in farm⁄houses sited at intervals along the dike

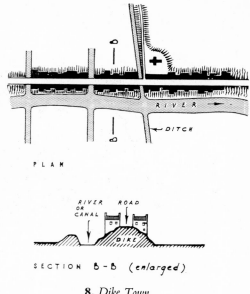

8. *Dike Town*

road, the spaces between them being gradually filled in with other habitations.

Although ribbon development is the least interesting form of Dutch town layout—many dike settlements are quite uninspired and thoroughly monotonous in appearance—it is nevertheless surprising how attractive it could become at the hands of mediaeval town builders. A slight variation in the usually straight alignment of the dike and a prominent feature such as a windmill to terminate the vista could result in a pleasant and interesting street picture, as seen in the village of Fijnaart, North Brabant. Where the dike ran alongside a wide water⁄way, the only alternative to extension of building along the dike was to use the lower ground protected by it. There was usually insufficient space on the berms of the dike for a large building such as a church, and this would in consequence take its place in the fields below (8). The church is so placed in Grootebroek, in Fijnaart and almost without exception in other old dike settlements. In the South Holland village of Moordrecht, single rows of houses on either side of the Hollandse⁄Ijssel dike form a narrow and slightly curved street; a small town hall is sited among the houses along the street but the church is on lower ground beside a minor road leading up from the fields to the town hall. Such an arrange⁄ment is both pleasing and rational, for it provides that the town hall, the symbol of secular authority, is situated amid the bustle of everyday life whilst the church

9. Sommelsdijk: typical dike street

stands slightly apart in a quiet, secluded place. The double town of Middel-harnis-Sommelsdijk on the island of Overflakkee demonstrates how the maximum use was made of safe building space on the dike (*9*).

Towns sited on dikes flanking a fairly narrow waterway afford an inte-resting variation on this theme of development. As in this case the waterway, the trade route, was virtually the lifeline of the town, houses were faced towards it thus giving rise to the familiar Dutch urban scene of a canal lined with buildings. The keys to success in such a composition lay in the width of the waterway and the length along which it was built up. If the waterway were too wide for a simple bridge, buildings on one side became isolated from those on the other and the "urban" effect was lost; if in addition building extended for more than a thousand yards or so in a straight line on either side, the effect was still worse: it deteriorated into mere characterless ribboning. Fortunately, in mediaeval foundations especially, this was not often the case, and some charming effects were achieved in the disposition of buildings along the waterfront.

The dike town established at the point where a land route crossed a waterway provides another variation in layout form. Here the two principal components, a built-up street and a built-up waterway, were in direct spatial contrast, and the opportunity was presented to the planner of complying with the simple tenet of design that the relationship between width of street and height of buildings should be such as to secure either a width well in excess of height, thus achieving a sense of spaciousness, or a width less than height, giving a sense of compactness as well as shade.

SLOTEN. That this tenet was well understood is shown in the little Friesland town of Sloten (town rights 1426). The main crossing, seen in the 1622 plan (*10*), is illustrated in the photograph (*11*). The church and adjoining parsonage are placed at the side of the tree-lined waterway whilst the town hall, a building of

SLOOTEN.

Wald brug

1. De Kerck
2. 't Raedthuys
3. Vis marckt
4. Groote steeg
5. Dubbel straat
6. Het Diep
7. Snacker poorte
8. Wald poorte
9. Lemster poorte
10. Wijcker poorte

10. *Sloten, 1622 (P. Feddes Harlingensis)*

11. *Sloten: road over canal, houses dated 1771 and 1764*

12. *Sloten: aerial view, courtesy K.L.M.*

no particular architectural significance, oc/
cupies one of the corners of the crossing.
A windmill by the eastern watergate and a
very fine tree at the western end complete
an extraordinarily satisfying urban com/
position, framed so impressively within its
broad defence moat (12).

NIEUWPOORT. One of the problems
of a cross/route plan of this kind was the
selection of suitable sites for the principal
buildings. At Nieuwpoort (1283), South
Holland, the town hall was built astride the
canal at the road crossing and the church
took a less prominent position along the
canal frontage (13, 14). The bridge was
widened to provide space for a small market
place, a device frequently adopted in Dutch
towns. Nieuwpoort is about the same size
as Sloten: it measures some 370 yards by
260 yards, the length of the canal within the

13. *Nieuwpoort: town hall astride canal, church
on canalside*

built/up area being the greater dimension. The present/day layout of this sleepy
little country town of barely 800 inhabitants is quite probably much the same
as it was six centuries ago but none of its original buildings survive; a great fire

14. *Nieuwpoort: canal scene and town hall*

in 1517 destroyed all but
six of the houses. The
two minor streets running
parallel with and on
either side of the canal
have never been paved
or fully developed with
buildings. The immense
fortifications, of which
the moats still remain,
belonged to the Renais/
sance era.

SCHOONHOVEN. A
third example of the

15. *Schoonhoven: canal scene and market shelter*

cross-route pattern is the rather larger town of Schoonhoven (*15*), on the north bank of the Lek opposite Nieuwpoort. It was set up *circa* 1280 by the local count to act, with nearby Gorinchem and the important commercial town of Gouda, as a rival of the thriving centre of Dordrecht. The basis of the layout was a built-up waterway crossed at right angles by two roads. The more important crossing was accentuated by siting the church and the market place on either side of it whilst the town hall with its slender, delicate spire had its place near the secondary crossing. This formed an exception to the usual practice of siting the town hall in close association with the market place and reserving a quieter setting for the church. The water-way was linked to an inner harbour and, via a sluice, to the Lek where a quay was constructed. Road access to the quay was also afforded via a town gate, which is the only one now surviving. Schoonhoven never achieved great success as a river port but has for centuries been a centre of activity for silversmiths. It, also, shows the marked contrast of scale between built-up streets and built-up canal and the dense planting greatly enhances the scene.

DIKE-AND-DAM TOWNS

Very characteristically Dutch layout forms are those of settlements originating at the site where a river or creek was dammed. The most famous of a long list of towns which developed in this way is Amsterdam. The stages of growth are indicated in the plan (*16*) which shows (*a*) a small dike settlement, and (*b*) the pattern resulting from the construction of the dam. The flow of the river was directed along alternative channels to the sea, the original downstream portion serving as an outer harbour and the upstream portion between the dam and the alternative channels as an inner harbour. The dikes constructed to define and contain the alternative channels provided the main circulation routes for land traffic, and on their berms were sited buildings directly concerned with external

41

trade such as warehouses and offices. The dam itself constituted a valuable central space and was treated as such; it provided the setting for public buildings like the town hall and weighing hall and, occasionally, a church. The "Dam" of Amsterdam has always been the civic centre and principal place of public assembly for the City. The lower ground lying between the streams was used for purposes less directly connected with external trade as, for example, shops, workshops, social buildings and houses; its layout form was in long, narrow blocks typical of the "water town" which will be referred to in Chapter IV.

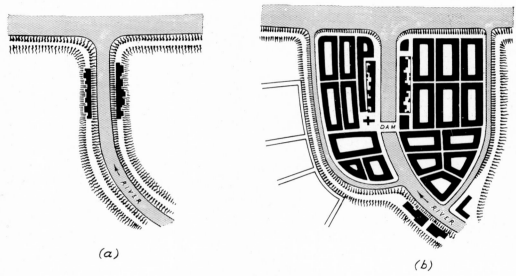

(a)

(b)

16. Dike-and-Dam Town: Amsterdam

A noticeable difference exists between the dike-and-dam towns of North Holland and those of the Zeeland archipelago. In the former several water routes were to be found within the town boundaries; in the latter there was usually only one, the dammed portion of the creek: there are no rivers on the islands. The placid, tree-lined urban canals so often seen in North Holland are absent in the island towns for the reason that their harbours were directly con-nected with the unpredictable waters of the sea or sea channels and it would have been dangerous to admit them. Also absent are the *vaarts*, the highway canals linking neighbouring towns and villages; intercommunication for Zeeland towns and villages was via the sea or overland.

17. *Zieriksee: town hall, fifteenth-century, tower 1550*

ZIERIKSEE, the chief town of Schouwen Island, like Middelburg the capital of Zeeland Province, is a good example of dike-and-dam town formation in the islands. Settlement took place there as early as the ninth century, when Zieriksee was a frontier post of the "Middle Kingdom".[2] It occupied slightly elevated ground lying near a sea channel, the Gouwe, that formerly separated the islands of Schouwen and Duiveland. At the beginning of the twelfth century a small township, consisting of a castle, a church dedicated to St. Lieven, a market place, a few houses and probably a town hall, was gaining prosperity by virtue of its accessible position in relation to traffic using the East Schelde route and its proximity to the more highly developed region of Flanders. Town rights were granted in 1248, and by that time the town had extended eastwards from the original nucleus, where the church now stands, along both sides of a diked creek leading to the Gouwe (18). A dam and two sluices were constructed across the creek to form harbour basins, and the flanking dikes provided sites for warehouses and other buildings serving overseas trade, whilst the old nucleus was given over to mainly local industrial activities such as weaving, salt-refining and the making of a red dye from plants grown locally. The area immediately west of the dam became the market, commercial and administrative centre; and the Flemish banking houses recorded as having been established in Zieriksee at the end of the thirteenth century were probably located there. During the fifteenth and sixteenth centuries its harbours were the base for the largest carrying fleet and herring fisheries in Zeeland, and great wealth came to the city; its new town hall built near the dam (17), its mighty gates and very large church are indicative of prosperity and prestige. Indeed, times were so good that the town council resolved in 1454 to give its church the highest tower in the world; but shortly afterwards a series of misfortunes—fires and floods, pestilence and political disfavour—prevented the realization of that ambition. The town suffered grievously

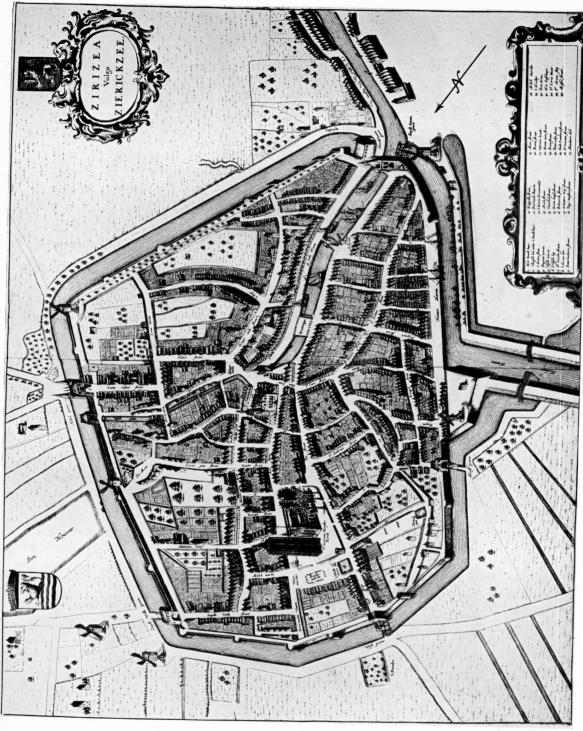

18. *Zierikzee, 1638* (J. Jansson)

during the Spanish occu-
pation of 1575–6, which
it had tried in vain to
avert by opening its dikes,
and it was not until the
end of the century that
something like its former
wealth and prestige was
restored. A great task had
to be achieved in order to
maintain prosperity: the
Gouwe, which was never
a very deep stream, had
sanded up gradually, and

19. *Zieriksee: panorama from approach-canal dike*

a new harbour and sea connection was needed; the Nieuwe Haven was therefore sited along the south-western fortification *singel*, and a long approach canal
about a mile in length, a portion of which is seen to the south of the plan (*18*)
and also in the photograph (*19*), was dug in 1597 to provide the necessary link
to the East Schelde. This new harbour became the centre of activity in overseas
trade; the Oude Haven frontages were thereafter used for merchants' houses
and offices, and the western part of it was filled in in 1767 to form a central
open space (*18*).

Comparison of the present-day layout plan with that shown on Jacob van
Deventer's map of *circa* 1560, or on Jansson's plan of 1638 (*18*), reveals very
little change in the city's size or the pattern and width of its narrow winding
streets; and much the same skyline is seen now (*19*) as in C. Pronk's engraving
of 1743.[3] Zieriksee declined in importance because it was too far removed from
the mainland and could not compete with the better sea routes enjoyed by
Amsterdam and Rotterdam. It functions now only in a local capacity as
administrative and market centre for Schouwen-Duiveland.

SEAPORTS

Not the least among geographical advantages enjoyed by other European
countries but denied to the Netherlands was the natural sea harbour. Apart
from a number of creeks, and these mostly shallow, the only refuges that ships
could find along her shores were those made by Dutchmen. From as early as the
fifth century, when Frisian sailors began to exploit the trade route to the Baltic,

45

Netherlanders must have appreciated that latent wealth lay seawards, in herring fishing and in the transport of merchandise, and that a homeland so meagrely endowed with natural resources could, of itself, yield nothing but the humblest means of livelihood for a small population. By early mediaeval times, Dutch merchants had invested

20. *Trier, Germany: town crane, 1413*

the rich profits accruing from herring fisheries in fleets of cargo ships, and had secured for themselves a leading position as carriers of Europe's goods and raw materials. The rapidly expanding volume of sea traffic created a demand for more and more harbour space and greater facilities for attendant activities such as shipbuilding and repairing, sailmaking, ropemaking and victualling, and also for increased warehouse and office accommodation.

The construction of a harbour entailed recessing the sea dike to form a loop, and dividing the space so formed into an outer harbour and one or more inner basins; these latter were controlled by sluices which admitted water at high tide and kept ships afloat at low tide. Constant dredging was also necessary. The zoning pattern of the typical seaport resembled that of the river port or dike-and-dam town: harbour frontages were reserved for merchants' offices, warehouses, shipbuilders' and repair yards, weighing hall and town crane, whilst church, town hall, shops and houses occupied lower ground behind the dikes. The town crane, just mentioned, was a familiar feature of any sea or river port in which heavy cargo had to be handled. It was built and managed by the local authority, who charged fees for its use. No old cranes survive in the Netherlands, but an interesting one may still be seen, for instance, at the German river port of Trier on the Moselle (*20*).

GOEREE. The layout of a mediaeval seaport is clearly seen in the island town of Goeree (*21*), situated on the eastern edge of a core of naturally high ground. A free translation of its Old Dutch name of Goedereede would be "a good pull-up for ships". A flourishing trading post as early as 1080, it received charter rights from Gerard van Voorne, Count of Zee-land, in 1312, and con-tinued to prosper until the sea approaches began to sand up towards the end of the fifteenth cen-tury. It happened that during the century a large-scale programme of land reclamation of near-by shallows was em-barked upon, and by the end of the seven-

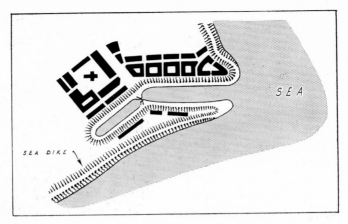

21. *Harbour Town: Goeree*

teenth century most of the modern island of Goeree-Overflakkee had come into being. The old port was thus left, high and practically dry, in the midst of agricultural land. Despite almost complete severance from seafaring activities, it still bears the characteristic stamp of a seaport, as does the stranded mediaeval port of Winchelsea in England. Broad cobbled quays lined with tall houses still look out on to the harbour basin; the town hall stands at the junction of the quay and the principal street; the massive square church tower, nowadays barely half its original height, is still a dominating landmark for most of the modern island; and proud if slightly shabby buildings attest to bygone wealth and prestige (*22*). Although the neighbouring village of Ouddorp is larger and more lively, Goeree with its population of only 1,100 is still accorded a somewhat matriarchal deference and retains social leadership in the original island area.

22. *Goeree: outer harbour and quays*

VEERE. A similar loop formation is to be seen at the little port of Veere (*23*) on the north-

23. *Veere, 1648 (Joannes Blaeu)*

east coast of Walcheren Island. Starting as a fishing settlement on a dike, it received charter rights from the lord of a neighbouring castle in the thirteenth century, and flourished as a seaport and fishing-fleet base over the succeeding four centuries. The northern dike, facing the sea, was constructed of massive proportions to protect

24. *Veere: quay scene*

both harbour and town. The southern dike acted as a quay and its frontage was developed with merchants' offices and houses and warehouses. The lower ground south of the quay was subdivided into building blocks by means of four streets leading downwards from the quay and others roughly parallel to it. One of the streets at right angles to the quay was made of sufficient width for a market to be held in it, but others were hardly more than twenty feet wide. It is noticeable that street entrances on to the quay were kept as narrow as practicable in order that *dijkplanken*, planks of wood, could be fitted across them to afford added protection against flooding in the event of abnormally high seas; these are a familiar feature of most seaports and of dike-and-dam towns near the open sea. The Gothic town hall, designed by Antoon Keldermans in 1474, was placed on the main street just below the quay, and forms a picturesque central feature of the urban complex as seen from the northern dike (*24, 25*). Its tower was added in 1599. The immense church (1479) had a site near the southern gate; it appears from *25* to be much smaller than it is in fact: it lies on lower ground than the town hall and about one hundred yards behind it (*23*). Veere enjoyed its period of greatest prosperity during the fifteenth century, when it had extensive trade with the Baltic countries as well as with Spain and Portugal, England and Scotland. The marriage in 1444 of one of its lords with a daughter of James I of Scotland forged a very strong commercial link with Scotland, particularly in the wool and cloth trade, which endured until late in the eighteenth century. The link is still commemorated in the "Scots' House", otherwise called "Het Lammetje" from the lamb emblem that

D   49

stands between the two principal windows at first-floor level. This building, standing on a prominent site along the quay, is an example of late Gothic architecture (1561) (25, 26). The sanding up of sea approaches towards the end of the seventeenth century brought economic disaster to the town. Its population dwindled

25. *Veere: Scots' House, town hall and church*

from some 8,000 in 1600 to barely a thousand at the present time. Its merchants were succeeded by fishermen and peasants; many of its houses, standing empty for years, were pulled down; its mighty fortifications were dismantled. The Kamperveerschepoort, guarding the harbour entrance, is the last remaining gate in this elegant little showpiece of late mediaeval town building.

BLOKZIJL, on the eastern coast of the former Zuider Zee, is not a town in the formal sense for it was never granted a charter, but it deserves mention here because the planning of its spacious harbour is so typical of mediaeval technique, and also because of the many delightful examples of early Renaissance buildings that it still possesses. It was only a small fishing hamlet before the fourteenth century but was planned as a seaport about 1500. The shape of the developed area was defined as a hexagon by the construction, in 1583, of a ring of fortifications in "Old Netherlands" style;[1] and of this area about one-third was taken up by the harbour

26. *Veere: façade of Scots' House, 1561*

50

itself. Harbour frontages were reserved for buildings mostly concerned with shipping trade, and church, shops and houses were located on secondary street running away from, or parallel to, the quays. The reclamation of a large area of the Zuider Zee, the North-East Polder, a few years ago has so completely severed the village from the water that it does not have even fishing boats; it acts instead as a local agricultural centre of very minor importance.

ENKHUISEN. The much larger port of Enkhuisen shows the typical loop formation, but had four inner basins controlled by sluices. Between 1580 and 1646 the number of inner basins had been increased to nine. The principal dike street, the Breestraat, was over 750 yards in length. A very wealthy past is exhibited in its fine gates, churches and merchant houses but in the late seventeenth century, in company with other formerly prosperous cities around the Zuider Zee coast, it became useless as a seaport and had to give place in overseas trade to ports more favourably situated.

*   *   *   *   *   *

Of town types discussed in this chapter only comparatively few achieved real standing in later times. Leiden and Gouda developed far beyond their dikes, as will be observed in Chapter IV; Amsterdam, Rotterdam and Middelburg rose to positions of leadership. Rotterdam was fortunate in its deep-water approaches and its situation as the natural entrepôt for merchandise from the hinterland and, even now, its prosperity is closely linked with that of Germany; Amsterdam, through sheer enterprise and foresight, kept open her vital connection with the sea by digging new approaches when existing routes became impracticable (see map 77); Middelburg retained mastery in the Zeeland archipelago when her rivals decayed, but enjoys little beyond a local influence. Many seaports which, up to the end of the seventeenth century, enjoyed worldwide fame and fortune, declined as a result of sanding up of their harbours and consequent inability to take ships of deeper draught. Goeree, Veere, Enkhuizen, and others like Brouwershaven on Schouwen, and Stavoren, Medemblik and Hoorn in the north virtually had the bottom knocked out of their economy, and their only contact with the water nowadays is the fishing fleet. There is something wistful about the ancient city of Hoorn, whose splendid architecture, the West-Friesland Government House (now Museum), town hall, weighing hall, gates, churches, hofjes, orphanages, doelen,[5] merchant houses and warehouses, display so impressively the glory of the "Golden Age", and the fame of whose sons still lives on: Tasman who discovered Tasmania and New Zealand, Schouten who sailed round the coasts of South America and gave the name of his city to the Cape, and Jan Pz. Coen who founded the Dutch East Indies. Dutchmen call these cities the "dode steden", the dead towns. Yet nowadays they are far from being lifeless monuments of a glorious history. They have indeed renounced the sea, from which they were irrevocably shut off in 1932 by the closing of the great Afsluitdijk linking North Holland and Friesland, but have turned towards the land to find a new, if less spectacular, prosperity as market and service centres.

REFERENCES

1. FOCKEMA ANDREAE, S. J., *Duizend Jaar Bouwen in Nederland*, 1948; PETERS, C. H., *op. cit.*, and others.
2. *Infra*, p. 115.
3. See BLAEU'S *Stedenatlas van de Vereenigde Nederlanden*.
4. See Chapter VI.
5. See Glossary.

CHAPTER III

Mediaeval Town Foundation
and Development: II

Bastides

THE widespread movement for founding new towns in Europe during the late thirteenth and early fourteenth centuries has been examined in detail by several authors.[1] In the first stages new towns were established in accordance with a pattern of military defence with the object of controlling newly acquired regions, but once these regions became fairly peacefully settled sound economic reasons emerged for building more towns to attract more settlers. Although the influence of the movement was felt also in the Netherlands its results there were nothing like so prolific as in France or Eastern Europe, and they occurred at a rather later date. Evidence exists that Count Floris V of Holland (1256–96), an adherent of, and frequent visitor to, France, had seen the extensive work of the brothers St. Louis, King of France, and Alfonse, Count of Poitiers, and their nephew King Edward I of England, and had introduced the idea of bastide-building into his own country.[2] The founding of the earliest Dutch examples, Arnemuyden (1288) and Brouwershaven (1285), in the Zeeland islands has been attributed to him; neither now survives in its original form.

Towns of this type were commissioned by minor Dutch nobles with the triple motive of protecting their domains, providing a market to attract trade, and raising their personal prestige. The marks of distinction of a French nobleman were the possession of a castle supplemented by a monastery, a hunting ground and a town; if his Dutch counterpart could not aspire to all these, he sought at least to control a town of his own. Some of the Dutch bastides, Vianen, Ijselstein, Culemborg, Montfoort, Bredevoort, Heusden and Helmond, were supplementary to a castle, and in this respect resembled those built by Edward I in Wales; others such as Elburg, Naarden and Kortgene were sited independently of the castle, as was often the case in the bastides of England and France.

53

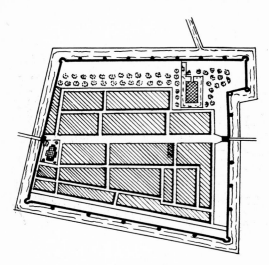

27. Vianen, 1744 (Based on plan by M. Bolstra)

In general the Dutch bastides do not bear the stamp of the French examples, which conformed very closely to a standardized plan: this consisted of a rectangular grid of narrow streets relieved by two central open spaces, one of which was the market, square in shape, surrounded by arcades and with the town hall set centrally along one of its sides, and the other, also square, was reserved for the church; the whole was surrounded by walled fortifications with powerful gates arranged as terminating features to the main streets. The Dutch counterpart displays no such standardization. The market place was seldom square and never colonnaded, and the church was rarely sited in such close proximity to it; markets were mostly held in wide streets, on widened bridges or alongside canals, and the church was usually placed well away from the busy commercial area. The only marked resemblances lie in the compactness of planning, the use of the rectangular pattern for street lines and the walled fortifications and gates.

VIANEN (1336), situated below the south bank of the Lek some twelve miles east of Nieuwpoort, illustrates appropriately the simplicity in layout characteristic of bastides. Its plan (27) shows it to be of approximately rectangular shape. The central axis, the broad straight High Street, is dominated at one end by the principal entrance to the town, the Lekpoort, and at the other by the tall church tower. The town hall is placed in this street, near the Lek gate, and acts as a terminating feature to one of the minor streets. The latter do not make direct crossings of the main road; the junctions are staggered so that street vistas are closed by main-road buildings. The plan provided no separate market place; stalls were erected along the middle of the High Street as was the custom in many an English market town. One other of the original gates survives: it is the sole remaining portion of the local ruler's castle, the former site of which is now, in the interests of progress, occupied by the municipal gasworks.

Of somewhat similar pattern is IJSELSTEIN (1331) on the north bank of the Lek a few miles from Vianen. Its town hall is centrally placed in the main longitudinal street, at the intersection with a cross-street leading from the castle, and is set back from the general building line of the main thoroughfare in order to make space for a small market place. The church, which has an early Renaissance tower of unusual design, stands in a quiet corner of the town beside the dike and moat.

28. *Culemborg: market place and town hall*

A rather later foundation in North Holland Province, PURMEREND (1410), resembles Ijselstein in having a central market place located at the intersection of the main north-south and east-west streets, but differs in that both town hall and church are sited in the square, the corners of which are closed by buildings.

29. *Culemborg: Hoogebinnenpoort, 1557*

CULEMBORG (or Kuilenburg), lying just below the south bank of the Lek in the fertile part of Gelderland Province called the Betuwe (meaning "good soil"), demonstrates the successful integration of a late thirteenth-century extension of bastide form with a nucleus of early twelfth-century date. As Blaeu's plan (*30*) indicates, the Lek dike was constructed at some distance from the river itself, and the intervening "graest uyter weyden", the outer meadows, were liable to flood during the winter months. The original town developed behind the dike and along both sides of a road which, coming from the Lek, divided into two branches inside the harbour gate (marked "havenpoort" on the plan). The building of a castle in

55

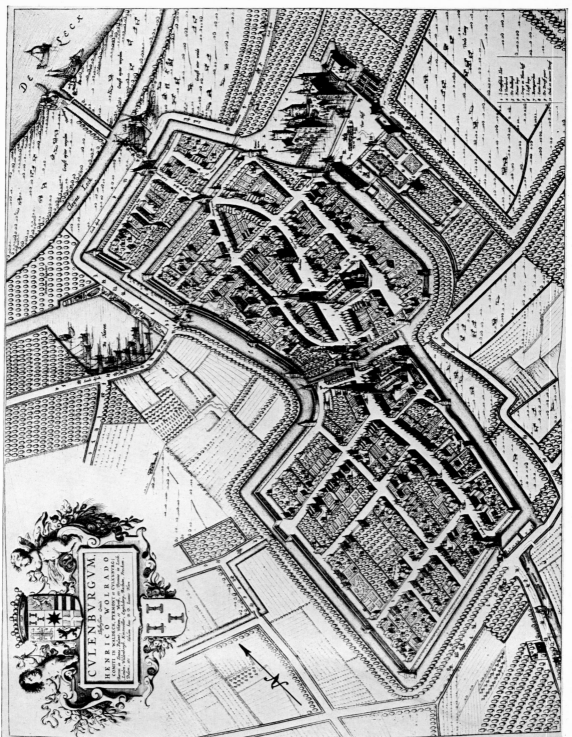

30. *Culemborg, 1648 (Joannes Blaeu)*

1271 and the grant of a charter in 1318 brought an increase in the town's importance and prosperity, and an extension, the "Nieuwstad", was made in a south-westerly direction during the years 1385–92. A satisfactory link between old and new towns was secured in the form of a road which passed from the market place (*29*) through the south gate (the Hoogebinnenpoort, *30*), and across the drainage canal. At about the same time a second, smaller, extension was made beyond the north-eastern boundary by reconstructing the Lek dike in U-shaped form.

It is evident from Blaeu's plan, which is dated 1648, that the second extension, the primary purpose of which was to make more commercial accommodation available, was fully utilized but that the increase of population for which the Nieuwstad was planned did not materialize: the density of development in this area is shown to be quite low and even today it is not greatly increased. The treatment of the market place and its three dominating features, the church, the town hall and the Hoogebinnenpoort, gave charm and grace to the old town. A sense of enclosure in the long, and for a Dutch town unusually wide, market place was successfully achieved by the continuity of its building frontages and the disposition of its terminating features, the gate, the town hall and the gentle curve of the street leading away from it to the harbour gate; and although in later times a row of shops built in front of the church reduced the size of the market place it still has a spacious appearance. Whilst the hub of interest lies, as it has always lain, in the old town, the Nieuwstad is no mere appendage: it unquestionably "belongs" to the whole town. The three parts are separated by canals but joined by roads; the inner gates do not shut out one part from another but invite access between them.

ELBURG. If a rival be sought to the neatness and symmetry of the French bastides, of which Montpazier is the most striking example, the little Gelderland town of Elburg has first place (*31*). It was functioning as a Zuider Zee port before 1230 and achieved town status in 1270, but little is known of the original foundation because it was completely rebuilt during the second half of the fourteenth century on a safer, slightly elevated, site further inland. The elements of the plan were an oblong of some 415 yards by 260 yards bisected about its shorter axis by a canal and divided into approximately rectangular blocks by narrow streets parallel with or at right angles to the canal. For the merchant and fishing fleets a broad quay was provided having its road connection with the town centre through the Vischpoort (*32*). As the new town was not primarily intended to attract trade from the hinterland it needed only a small market place, and space for it was obtained by increasing the width of canal bridge at the central crossing point, as was done at Nieuwpoort and elsewhere. The church was placed, as at Ijselstein, in a secluded corner and a plot was allotted in the south-eastern quarter for a monastery and chapel. The rather insignificant town hall owes its equally insignificant site, on one of the minor streets parallel to the canal, to the fact that it was formerly a house belonging to the Count of Gelderland and existed before the town was planned. The mediaeval town walls with their twenty half-round

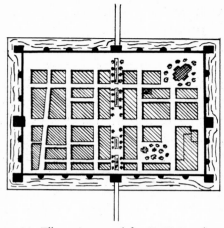

31. *Elburg, circa 1579 (after C. H. Peters)*

towers, four gates and four corner towers enclosed an area of some sixty acres.

As an urban composition Elburg has appeal not because its features are outstandingly beautiful but because they are in harmony and yet show sufficient contrast to provide visual interest, and because the layout as a whole displays a logical regularity. The central tree-lined canal (*33*), flanked by buildings of unified though not uniform architectural character, is in marked spatial contrast with the narrow streets of diverse architectural styles which lead to it. Street vistas were, and in some cases still are, pleasantly closed by suitable features (*32, 34*). Occasional added interest is afforded at ground level by *keienstoepjes* or mosaic pebble pavements of various patterns as shown in the right foreground in photograph *34*. Generous tree planting on the site of former fortifications has resulted in a pleasant and popular promenade. Only a few years ago the town still looked out over the broad expanse of the former Zuider Zee. Now it looks out to the polder dikes that will soon surround nearly a quarter of a million acres

32. *Elburg: Vischpoort, 1592*

33. *Elburg: canal and seventeenth-century gables*

of reclaimed sea bed. The eel-fishing industry will in consequence be severely curtailed, but the reclamation plan has provided for retention of a water route to what will remain of the Ysselmeer, so that some of Elburg's fishermen can still go down to the lake in ships.

NAARDEN (35), like Elburg, started as a fishing and trading port on the Zuider Zee shore but, after a fire in 1350, was rebuilt at the order of Count Willem V as a "nieuwestad" on higher ground about a thousand yards further inland, the approach canal to the harbour being extended accordingly. The plan comprised an approximately rectangular grid of streets of some twenty feet width with the main street across the shorter axis. In contrast with the usual layout pattern of Dutch towns, the great church of St. Vitus, which was commenced in 1380 and took sixty years to complete, was sited in a central square just off the main street. Immediately west of it, on the opposite side of the street, another open space of about two acres was reserved as a market place. Naarden's market function cannot have been very important, however, for the space was gradually covered by encroaching buildings until practically none of it remained. Thus the two central open spaces which the town, in common with bastides in general, was intended to possess, have all but disappeared. The town hall (36), a characteristic example of early Renaissance architecture (1601), was

34. *Elburg: side street with* keienstoepjes *and church*

59

one of the buildings that encroached upon the original market place. Naarden had secured considerable wealth by the fifteenth century, and had a large fishing and carrying fleet as well as important weaving and velvet-making industries. In 1572 the town and its people suffered terrible savagery at the hands of the Spaniards, but by the turn of the century it had made a good recovery if the town hall, church and patrician houses along the Kloosterstraat are any criterion. In the seventeenth

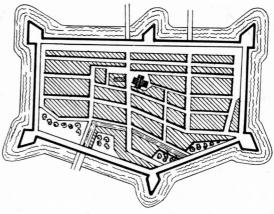

35. Naarden, 1632 (Based on plan by M. Boxhoorn)

century its vital strategic position caused it to be developed as a fortress in the national defence pattern. The fortifications shown on plan 35, which is drawn from an early seventeenth-century town map, were replaced during the years

36. Naarden: town hall, 1601

1673–85 by mighty installations in the Vauban style, comprising six great bastions and ravelins set in wide moats, protected gun emplacements and enfilade firing points and a vast network of covered routes and passages connecting armouries and ammunition stores to firing positions. The superstructure was dismantled during the nineteenth century, but the outlines of rampart and moat, as seen from the air, still present a most formidable appearance (37).

VOLLENHOVE. Mention should be made of the charming mediaeval town Vollenhove, planned in 1354 as a *nieuwestad* appendage to a bishopric and tucked behind what was once the eastern dike of the Zuider Zee. The placing of the market square, with its church and town hall, was of interest in that it lay just below the dike, thus gaining emphasis as the principal

37. Naarden: aerial view, courtesy K.L.M.

entrance to the town from the harbour and, at the same time, claiming additional importance in that the principal streets led the bulk of traffic to and from the harbour through it. Many well preserved early seventeenth-century buildings (*38*) give an air of grace and maturity to a sleepy little town which, like Blokzijl, is now completely dissociated from the means of livelihood that brought its former prosperity.

*   *   *   *   *   *

The vigorous campaign for founding new towns in mediaeval Europe produced impressive results numerically: Germany, Poland and Czechoslovakia,[3] as well as South-West France, are literally strewn with them. But the bastide that grew to major importance in modern times is a comparative rarity. Hull, Breslau, Vilna, Strasbourg and Carcassonne are among the few exceptions. Many were founded as land-settlement speculations and some as rivals to estab-

38. Vollenhove: former Latin School, 1627

lished trading centres, but most had as their *raison d'être* a function in a particular scheme of military defence. When the course of events rendered that scheme obsolete, its components had to justify their continued existence in the pattern of local and regional market and administrative centres. Few succeeded in achieving much beyond minor town status (Neuenstadt in Switzerland and Granzee in Brandenburg are pleasant examples whose layout still accords with plans prepared six and a half centuries ago); most remain as mere villages and many in South-West France disappeared altogether, leaving no trace of their former sites.[4]

As for the Dutch bastides, if none can be said to have achieved conspicuous success few can be classed as failures. Two of them, Arnemuyden close to Middelburg and Kortgene (Noord-Beveland), were destroyed by the sea and rebuilt on other sites; another, Brouwershaven, lost its harbour approaches to shifting sands; but most were overshadowed economically by more powerful neighbours. On the whole the survivors manage to play an energetic, if limited, local part in the present-day social and economic pattern of Dutch urban life.

If they can be said to have any claim to fame, it is as living representatives of the golden age of mediaeval new-town planning.

REFERENCES

1. TOUT, T. F., *op. cit.*; GIRY, A., article on bastides in *La Grande Encyclopedie*; BERNOULLI, HANS, *Die Stadt und ihr Boden*, 1946.
2. PETERS, C. H., *op. cit.*, Vol. I, p. 192.
3. BERNOULLI, HANS, *op. cit.*, includes maps showing their locations, pp. 40–1.
4. TOUT, T. F., *op. cit.*, p. 14.

CHAPTER IV

Mediaeval Town Foundation and Development: III

Water Towns and Geestgrond Towns

WATER TOWNS

AMONG the many interesting, and indeed one may say unique, town types of the Netherlands, there is one that stands foremost in the expression of national urban characteristics. Dutchmen call it the *grachtenstad*, the water town, built largely upon land reclaimed from marsh or lake. The best examples are found in the provinces of North and South Holland, although some are also to be seen in Friesland and Groningen. They started usually as trading posts, clinging to small areas of firm ground slightly higher in level than the surrounding country-side or to dikes constructed alongside a navigable waterway. When increased trading and industrial activity forced them to expand they could only do so by developing land which, in its natural state, was quite unsuitable for the pur-pose (plan *39*).

The process of expansion was attended by many difficulties. A decision had first to be reached on the amount of extra land likely to be required to meet the needs of the town for the next few generations. Then came the engineering problems of removal and control of surplus water and of the maintenance of a constant level for canal water within the town. This entailed the digging of a wide encircling moat and, leading to it across the area, a series of narrower, parallel drainage canals (*grachten*). Sluices and, later, windmill pumps had also to be installed to remove surplus water from the canals to a tidal river. Finally the new land had to be raised above flood level, consolidated and made fit for building. Spoil excavated from new canals was used for this purpose, but often sand had to be brought from considerable distances to supplement local materials; Haarlem merchants found it profitable to win sand from the River Spaarne and transport it by barge to towns on even lower land which needed to prepare more

64

land for building. Deep pile foundations had also to be made for major buildings such as town halls, guild halls, weighing halls and churches. Whilst the primary purpose of the canals was that of drainage they had other functions besides: the encircling canal acted as defence moat, and grachten provided means of access to building frontages and ways of communication within the town. It is hardly necessary to observe that where land had to be so laboriously reclaimed, raised,

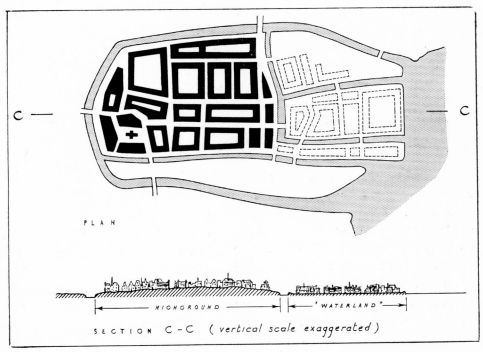

PLAN

HIGHGROUND   'WATERLAND'

SECTION C-C (vertical scale exaggerated)

39. *Water Town: Alkmaar*

drained and defended, there could be no question of casual development. No *grachtensteden* can be placed in the "chance-grown" category. The cost of preparation demanded the best possible use of land, and this could only be secured by strict adherence to a detailed town plan.

The resulting town showed an orderly, compact layout. Space was seldom available for wide streets, large market places, extensive forecourts to prominent buildings or amenity purposes. All canal-side frontages were closely developed; those along wider waterways were reserved for important commercial and resi-

40. *Delft: Oude Delft and ordnance warehouse, 1692*

41. *Delft: Oude Delft and Oude Kerk*

dential purposes, whilst industrial uses and houses for lower-paid workers took their place along narrower canals. Industrial and warehouse accommodation was often built up to the waters' edge (*40*) to enable easier loading and unloading of barges, but normally a narrow cobbled street, seldom exceeding twenty feet in width, was provided on either side of the waterway to give pedestrian, and later vehicular, access to buildings. At intervals along the frontage, space was allowed for narrow lanes (*steeg*) to effect lateral communication. In mediaeval times canals were crossed by means of wooden bridges; it was not until the seventeenth century that these were replaced by the now familiar stone arched type. Generous tree-planting acted as a foil to the straightness and regularity of waterways that might otherwise have proved monotonous (*41*).

*　　　*　　　*　　　*　　　*　　　*

DELFT. The classic example of the *grachtenstad* is Delft, which takes its name from the *delf* or ditch dug probably during the ninth century to connect the rivers Vliet and Schie. A small settlement had formed along its banks at a very early date, but it was entirely replanned during the thirteenth century and received a charter from William II, Count of Holland, in 1246. The basic pattern of the development was determined by three waterways: the Oude Delft, the original delf, the Nieuwe Delft which was cut parallel to and some seventy yards east of the Oude Delft, and a natural waterway which ran diagonally across the field drainage canals and then turned in a northerly direction parallel with the other two, as shown in Blaeu's plan (*42*). The first town, enclosed *circa* 1300 by a wall, contained a church, the Oude Kerk, a castle belonging to the Counts of Holland, a gasthuis and some hofjes, warehouses and workshops and the usual complement of shops and houses.

The city's earliest function was that of market for the dairy produce of the surrounding countryside. Count Floris V, however, wished to see industrial development there and as a result of his encouragement the brewing of beer, based on imported grain, became well established during the latter part of the thirteenth century. Records exist of the Count's orders (1274) concerning the sale of hops and the period over which beer had to be stored before sale.[1] By the middle of the fourteenth century this venture had met with such success that markets in Flanders and Brabant were captured from German cities. The need for a better connection to the sea and for harbour facilities for larger ships soon became apparent, and the City Council therefore had the River Schie, which at that time flowed into the mouth of the Rhine, canalized and deepened, and built a special port, Delfshaven, on the north bank of the Rhine to deal with the expanding volume of trade. The cloth industry also began to make headway following the settling in Delft of Flemish weavers who worked with wool imported from England. The location of this industry is shown by such place-names as Verversdijk (dyers' dike), Voldersgracht (fullers' ditch) and Raamstraat (loom street).

Continued expansion of industrial activity called for more land to be brought into development, and about 1350 an eastward extension beyond the Verversdijk, which had been constructed to control the natural waterway, nearly doubled the city's area. Former field drainage ditches now acted as grachten and reclaimed fields were divided into long, narrow, rectangular building blocks characteristic of the water towns. Important changes also took place in the central area. The castle was converted into the town hall (*43*) and its gardens provided the site for

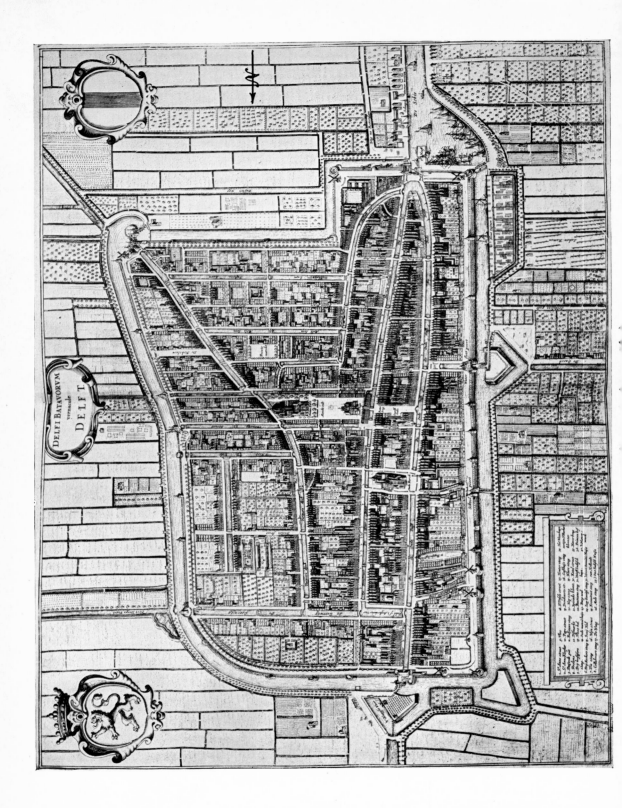

DELFI BATAVORVM vernacule DELFT

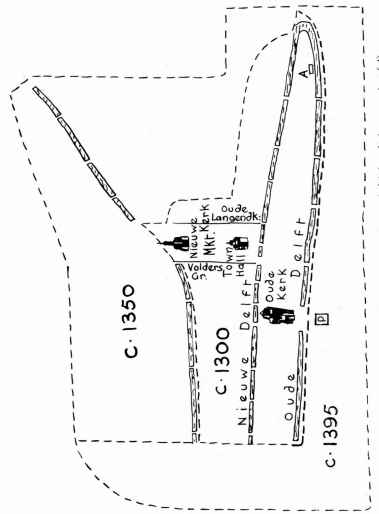

c·1350

c·1300

Nieuwe Delft

Oude Delft

c·1395

Volders
Gr.

Nieuwe Mkt. Kerk

Oude
Langendk.

Town
Hall

Oude Kerk

Delft

A

P

42a. Delft. Key to 42, showing also subsequent sites of Prinsenhof (P) and Armamentarium (A)

43. *Delft: market place and town hall, remodelled, 1618 (from the Nieuwe Kerk)*

the market place. The latter was unusually large, particularly for a water town, and now appears even larger because the lofty spire of the Nieuwe Kerk, begun in 1381, dwarfs the houses and shops surrounding it. These buildings had no gardens; they backed on to canals, the Oude Langendijk and the Voldersgracht, formed from the moat of the castle (*43, 44*). Further extensions to the west and north, commenced about 1395, produced equally orderly development and made Delft the third largest town in Holland at that time. Its world-famous faience pottery industry was introduced towards the end of the sixteenth century.

It should be observed that such extensions did not always result in the space which they enclosed being built up within a few years; on the contrary, as early town maps indicate, the drainage and encircling canals were dug first, later the walls and gates were added, and then the town gradually spread outwards within the enceinte. Miscalculations of the future needs in population and industry were sometimes made; this happened with Delft, which became overshadowed in industrial importance by Leiden, Haarlem and Gouda so that its later extensions were not fully developed for some centuries. It was, nevertheless, a wise policy to allow for extensions greater than the estimated increase of population seemed to warrant,

44. *Delft: Voldersgracht and Nieuwe Kerk tower*

for towns were often subject to siege and an area of open land within the walls proved of value in such an emergency. There is evidence, for example, at Breda,[2] that neighbouring villages were called upon to pay their share of the cost of extending the city walls in return for the shelter they could expect in times of attack.

A terrible fire in 1536 laid waste about two-thirds of the city of Delft, so that few buildings of earlier date survive, but the two principal churches escaped destruction and were completed in their present form by the end of the sixteenth century. Rebuilding proceeded in accordance with the same town layout, however, for it was largely determined by the existing pattern of canals and the position of usable piling foundations. A remarkable building which dates from before the fire is the former monastery of St. Agatha, which after the Reformation was used as the town house of William the Silent and later the Cloth Makers' Hall. The seventeenth century saw some very fine architectural achievements: Hendrik de Keyser remodelled the town hall, retaining the Gothic tower that remained from the original house of the Counts of Holland; the Corn Exchange, the "Butter House" and several other buildings in and around the market place added distinction to the central area; two hofjes were rebuilt; and frontages to the larger canals were graced by lofty and beautifully proportioned houses, offices and warehouses of which the Gemeenlandshuis, the offices of the East India Company (now used by the Technical High School) and the Armamentarium (40) are excellent examples.

Delft remains one of the loveliest of old Dutch cities although considerable industrial expansion has taken place outside its moat in recent years. Its greatest attraction lies in the repose and dignity of shaded canals lined with continuous façades of stately old houses, eloquent indeed of the tenet that the street should be regarded as a single architectural composition. It offers no guidance in problems of road traffic circulation, for which it was never designed, except to point to the pleasure of living practically without it. The city is sufficiently small to enable everyday life to be carried on with no great inconvenience on a pedestrian or cyclist basis, and its streets are vivacious and busy. Canalside roads are too narrow to permit of more than the occasional car or lorry, and excessive speed is physically impossible. Its spacious market square, dominated by the Nieuwe Kerk at one end and the handsome town hall at the other, is lined with attractive old shops, many still in their sixteenth- and seventeenth-century form but managing, nevertheless, to meet the needs of twentieth-century shoppers. Its commanding church spires, that of the Oude Kerk leaning heavily several degrees from the vertical (*41*), and the sole surviving gate, the Oost-poort, make a noble contribution to a particularly delightful townscape. In silhouette the city still presents something of the dignity, grace and maturity that Vermeer captured in his "View of Delft" though the Rotterdam-schepoort which he portrayed has since been demolished.

45. Leiden: Burcht, town hall tower at left

LEIDEN. In its three phases of development this famous old city illustrates three essentially Dutch layout forms: it was successively a burcht, a dike town and a water town. It is said to have been a trading post in Roman times[3] but Dutch authorities do not support this contention.[4] Whatever its origin may have been there is little doubt that its site at the confluence of three rivers, the Old and New Rhines and the Mare, was destined for importance. The burcht (*45*) was founded upon slightly elevated ground between the Rhine branches, an excellent place for defence purposes and for commanding the neighbouring terrain. The summit, crowned by a brick wall dating from 1300 enclosing an area of about a quarter of an acre, served as a temporary refuge in times of attack for the inhabitants of the wooden houses clustering at its base.

The city early found favour with the Counts of Holland; it was the birthplace of two of them, William II (1228) and Floris V (1256), and the interest shown by these powerful rulers assured its political and economic progress. The first planned extension, as shown on Blaeu's plan (*46*) and key, started early in the thirteenth century with the building of the Breestraat, a curved street some 750 yards long, on the prolongation of the dike controlling the New Rhine. This was a typical dike street with insufficient depth on its berms for large buildings, so that the church, St. Pieterskerk, and the Gravensteen, a residence of the Counts of Holland, were sited on the lower ground protected by it. The date of its charter is not known; it has been put as early as 1186 and certainly not later than 1266, when its citizens were granted the privilege of constructing a defence wall and moat on the line of the present Rapenburg.

The fortified area was built up in less than a lifetime, for in 1294 a second extension took place to the south of the Burcht. This introduced the true character of the grachtenstad; four parallel canals, the most northerly being later drained to form a street, and one street, the Middelweg, all intersected by a series of narrow lanes, subdivided the reclaimed land. The new wall followed the line of the present Vestestraat, and another church, the Hooglandskerk, was built near the Burcht. Development within this extension was of a spacious character, as the place-names Hooi(hay)gracht and Groene(green)steeg suggest, and has remained so throughout the centuries.

The broadcloth industry, already fostered by the Counts, expanded rapidly during the fourteenth century when weavers from Ypres found refuge in the city. The manufacture of baize and camlet was also embarked upon, and the success which attended these activities necessitated further living and working space. The third extension, started in 1355, followed much the same pattern as the first: another encircling canal was dug; another long dike street, the Haarlemmerstraat, was constructed on the prolongation of a river dike, the Old Rhine in this case; and another church was built on the lower ground behind it. The new area, primarily intended for workshops and artisans' houses, was developed hastily to a high density and a low standard and has retained its original character ever since. A fourth enlargement, west and south of the Rapenburg, was commenced in 1389 and took over thirty years to complete. The layout form was typical of a grachtenstad, with canals as the chief routes of communication, long and shallow building blocks, few and narrow streets and a broad *singel* enclosing the area. By the beginning of the fifteenth century Leiden had become the largest town in the Netherlands; its population exceeded 10,000.

Hofjes were well in evidence in the city as they were, and still are, all over the Netherlands: Leiden had about twenty out of a total of some two hundred in the country. As they form such a pleasant and characteristic feature in the make-up of Dutch towns a digression is here made to describe them.[5] The desire to help the poor and the aged first took expression in the building of gasthuisen, in which sick and aged were nursed by religious orders and the needy could find a meal and a bed. Town councils also set up *proveniershuisen* to meet such needs, but the greatest contribution came from private individuals who made gifts or bequests for establishing hofjes. Before the Reformation it was the custom to bequeath money or property for this kind of charity to the Holy Ghost, the funds being administered by the "Holy Ghost Masters"; hence the name "Heelige Geesthofje" that still survives in several towns. A foundation

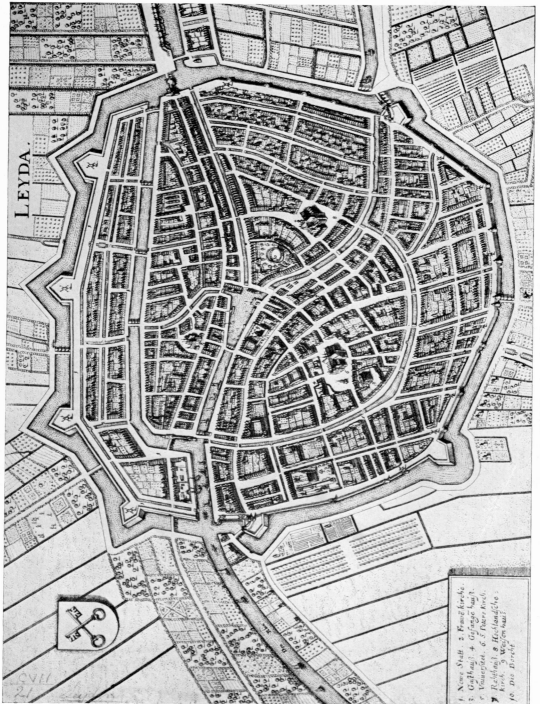

LEYDA.

1. Newe Statt   2. Fraw kirche.
3. Gasthaus.   4. Gefange haus.
5. Vauserstat.   6. S. Peters kirch.
7. Rathhaus.   8. Hochlandsche-
kirch.   9. Weijen haus
10. Die Borcht

46. Leiden, circa 1640 (Joannes Blaeu)

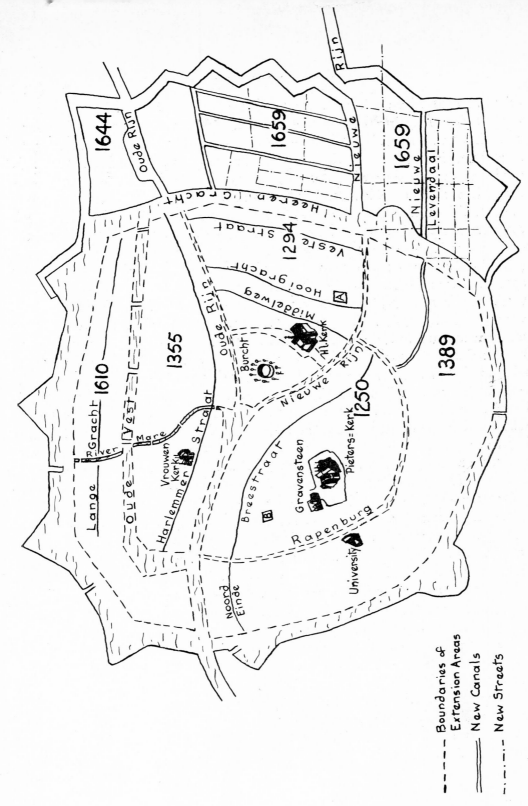

46a. Leiden. Key to 46. A, St. Anna Hofje; B, van Brouwckhoven Hofje

Boundaries of Extension Areas
New Canals
New Streets

1644
1659
1659
Oude Rijn
Nieuwe
Nieuwe
Levendaal
Heeren Gracht
Veste Straat
1294
Hooigracht
Middelweg
1355
1610
Oude Rijn
Burcht
Nieuwe Rijn
H.Kerk
Lange R.Gracht
Oude Vest
Mare
River
Vrouwen Kerk
Harlemmen Straat
Breestraat
Gravensteen
Pieters-Kerk
1250
1389
Rapenburg
University
Noord Einde

of similar kind was the *bagijnhof*, consisting of small houses built in cloister form, in which lay women could devote themselves to a religious life. Both existed from early times: Breda had the earliest bagijnhof (1240) and Utrecht the first hofje (1357). After the Reformation most bagijnhoven were dissolved, rendering many women homeless,

47. *Leiden: St. Anna Hofje and chapel, circa 1500*

but the charitable disposition of Dutch citizens was not affected by changes in religious beliefs and many new hofjes were set up during the seventeenth and eighteenth centuries. Bequests for their foundation were administered by trustees or *regenten*, who were obliged to adhere strictly to the wishes of the testator even when such were of an eccentric nature. In modern times, as in centuries gone by, the trustees still meet to conduct the affairs of the hofje in the *regentenkamer*, a stately and handsomely appointed room whose oil paintings reflect the wealth and style of the period in which the founder lived.

Occasionally hofjes were built in terraces along a street and sometimes on three sides of a quadrangle with a low wall and railings along the fourth side, the street frontage. The most usual layout form, however, was that of short terraces arranged in precinct fashion around a courtyard, entered from the street through an unobtrusive arched gateway. For a composition in which the aim was to achieve a sense of quietude and peaceful seclusion, the treatment of the enclosed space, with its restful continuity of façade, well-tended garden, ornamental pump and, sometimes, its own small chapel, could hardly have been bettered. Lying only a few paces from a busy street or quay, hofjes nevertheless give the impression of being far removed from the noise and the cares of the outside world (*47, 48*). Some of the eighteenth-century foundations lack the qualities of friendliness and intimacy of those of earlier times, and exhibit a somewhat ostentatious form of charity with disproportionate wealth lavished upon the entrance portals and regentenkamer. Teylers Hofje (1787) in Haarlem, a monument to a wealthy benefactor of the city, is an example of formal, classical design which misses

48. *Leiden: Van Brouwckhoven Hofje, 1640*

these qualities and conveys, instead, a rather forbidding and certainly draughty welcome to its occupants.

Another feature of interest that Leiden shares with many other old Dutch cities, including Haarlem (56) and Amersfoort (67), lies in the terraces of small houses, and sometimes shops, which back on to the walls of its old churches or nestle between their buttresses. To foreign eyes it seems a somewhat inappropriate use of holy ground. The houses usually accommodated church employees, among whom were the *stovenzetsters*, the women whose curious occupation it was to ensure that *stoven* or footwarmers were charged with charcoal so that their owners could give closer attention than might otherwise have been the case to long services in unheated churches.

A very good impression of Leiden as it must have appeared in late mediaeval times is gained from the area enclosed within the first extension. The great bulk and height of St. Pieterskerk are predominant in the scene. Narrow lanes lead down from the high Breestraat to the enclosed space in which the Pieterskerk stands, and thence to the broad Rapenburg. The Gravensteen, which backs on to the church square, looks out on to another enclosed square. The building was enlarged several times during the fourteenth and fifteenth centuries, and in the sixteenth century it housed the law courts and prison; its northern façade incorporated a screen behind which, from a position of dignity and comparative safety, magistrates could watch justice being done upon offenders in the execution square.[6]

Further extensions to the city will be noted in Chapter VII but it may be observed here that, despite its mellow and gracious appearance, Leiden is rather a formless aggregation. Unlike Delft, but in common with many towns of dike origin that developed as grachtensteden, it lacks a strongly defined centre. It possesses no large market place though several small ones are sited alongside broad waterways or on bridges astride them (50). The town hall, designed by

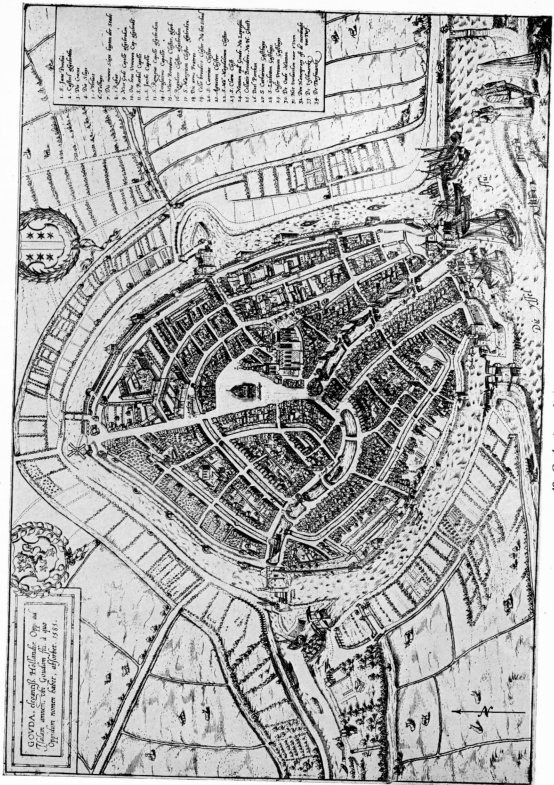

49. *Gouda, circa 1585 (Braun and Hogenberg)*

50. *Leiden: New Rhine, bridge market, town hall to left*

51. *Leiden: Rapenburg, University Hall to left*

Lieven de Key, a building of great beauty which was destroyed by fire in 1929 but whose façade was restored in the original design, stands in dike-town tradition along the Breestraat. A former nunnery, the White Nun Chapel, later housed the oldest of Dutch universities, founded in 1575 by William the Silent in recognition of the gallant resistance offered by Leideners to long siege by the Spaniards. As befits a university town, the seat of learning enjoys a setting of repose and dignity beside the placid waters of the Rapenburg (*51*).

GOUDA. The site of this old river port presented a physical planning problem of unusual interest which, in course of time, was successfully solved. The first nucleus was grouped around a castle built at the point where the meandering river Gouwe met the broad Hollandse Ijssel, and it developed north-westwards along the Gouwe dikes. In Braun and Hogenberg's plan (*49*) the Ijssel is seen to the lower right. The settlement achieved sufficient importance to merit the granting of a charter in 1272. Like Delft, it acted as a market for local dairy produce; Gouda cheeses are still world famous. The first manufacturing industries, brewing and weaving, expanded at a rate similar to those of Delft and Leiden, and town extension was therefore necessitated towards the middle of the fourteenth century. The unusual elements that had to be taken into account in the development plan were a right-angled bend in the Gouwe, two straight roads coming in from the fields to meet at an angle of 60 degrees near this bend and, between the roads, a large triangular space which had been presented by the Lord of Gouwe to form a market place for his town. The integration of these three features in the plan pro-

52. *Gouda: the Gouwe and St. Janskerk, covered market at right*

duced, ultimately, a town centre of beauty and strength of form. The first church of St. Jan was sited near the bend of the Gouwe and the meeting-point of the field roads, but its northern façade was not permitted to take up valuable

53. *Gouda: town hall, 1449-57, rebuilt 1690*

shopping frontage; shops were built on all market frontages, and the field road run-ning northwards was developed as a main thoroughfare along its western flank. The town hall was given an unusual position in the middle of the market place with the weighing hall (by Pieter Post, 1668) directly behind it on the periphery. Photo-graph 52 shows the gentle rise in the street towards the Gouwe dike and St. Janskerk, rebuilt in 1552 after a fire, and 53 the delicate Gothic town hall, built 1449-59 and rebuilt in 1690, as seen from the southern apex of the market.

Later extensions outwards from the mar-ket place were strictly in the water town tradition, regular, orderly and with a series of grachten as the essential preliminary to development in each case. It is recorded that up till the middle of the eighteenth

80

century there was no house of any consequence in the city that did not have its own connection by water to the Gouwe,[7] but by the middle of the following century many of the waterways had been drained and built up to form carriage-ways. Gouda, again like Delft, is an exception to the generality that water towns have no large market place: it boasts the biggest in Holland.

GEESTGROND TOWNS

The towns built partly on firm ground and partly on "waterland" show an interesting contrast in the treatment of the two parts: some degree of informality of development is evident on the higher ground whilst the lower bears every sign of premeditated layout and strict control. Haarlem and Alkmaar, among others, demonstrate the contrast well.

HAARLEM resembles Leiden in being a "town of many parts": originating as a stronghold at the time of the Danish invasions, it developed in the twelfth century as the supplement to a castle, in the thirteenth and fourteenth as a geest-grond town, and in the fifteenth and seventeenth centuries as a water town.

The first nucleus (see Thomaszoon's map, 54) was located on high ground at a bend in the river Spaarne where the castle, the Bakenesse, was built, its vulner-able western flank being protected by a canal, the Bakenessegracht, dug during the thirteenth century. The site was easily defensible, surrounded by fertile fields and lush meadows, readily accessible to the hunting grounds of the Haarlem forest lying to the south, and within easy reach of the main overland route through Holland Province which ran north and south across firm, sandy ground some three hundred yards west of the Bakenessegracht. It was, therefore, a natural choice for the principal residence of the Counts of Holland, who made it their headquarters from the eleventh to the thirteenth centuries. Town rights were granted by Count Willem II in 1245.

The original site soon proved too limited for the growing settlement, and as a suitable area of geestgrond lay westwards from the Bakenessegracht a new and more spacious town began to take shape there early in the thirteenth century, gaining in prosperity from its situation astride the meeting-point of the Spaarne river traffic and the overland trade route to North Holland. Early growth was concentrated in two places: one was the river harbour, on the bend of the Spaarne where it met the geestgrond and where the weighing hall still stands; and the other a large open space, thought to be a tournament field originally, surrounded by knights' houses. These two places were connected by an east-west street, the Damstraat, about a hundred yards long. The open space functioned as a market

F

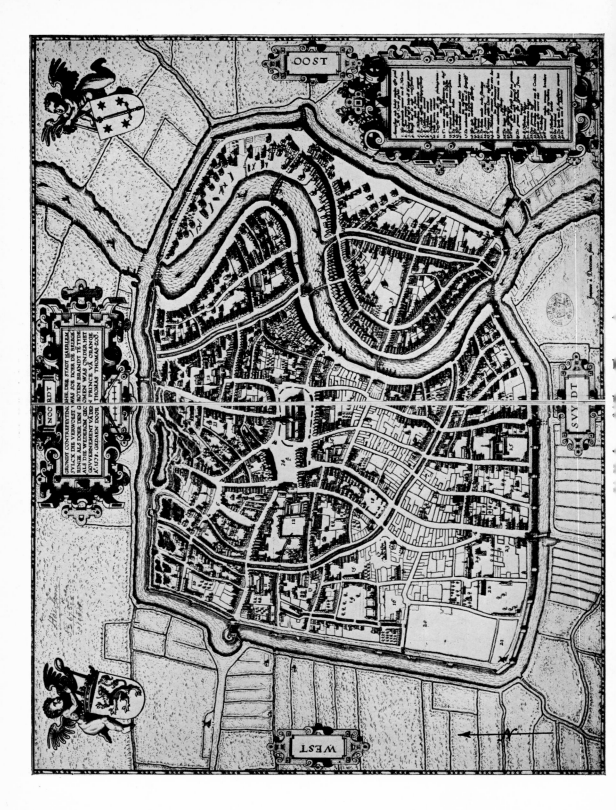

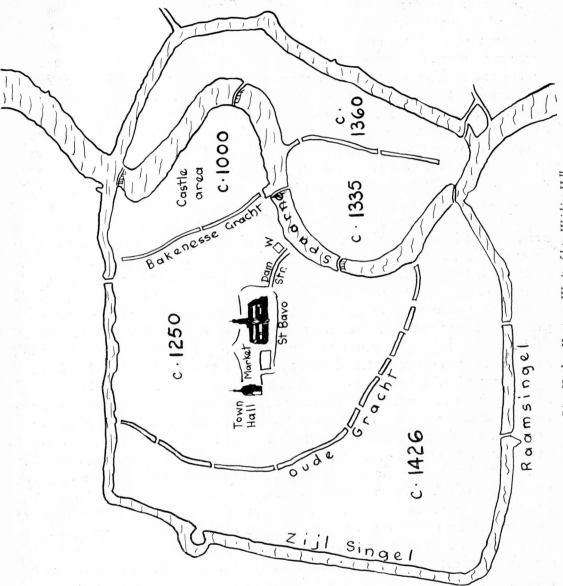

Castle area c·1000

c·1360

c·1335

Bakenesse Gracht

Spaarne Str.

Dam W.

St Bavo

Market

Town Hall

c·1250

Oude Gracht

c·1426

Raamsingel

Zijl Singel

54a. Haarlem. Key to 54. W, site of later Weighing Hall

83

place, and a house on its western flank which formerly belonged to the Counts of Holland was taken into use as the town hall; other former knights' houses became used as shops; and St. Bavo church started to develop on the south-eastern portion of the space. Of the various paths that meandered across the geestgrond to this open space, ten eventually became streets. Growth of the town around these features was spontaneous and haphazard; the only component of it that can have been planned was the defence wall and moat, which enclosed an area of some 220 acres (see key to 54). Two smaller extensions, in 1335 and 1360, were made on geestgrond slightly above flood level and therefore presented no problems of land drainage and consolidation. As with the first extension, development there amounted to little more than casual infilling of street frontages as demand arose.

The city's chief economic activities in mediaeval times were brewing, weaving and shipbuilding; its important market-gardening and horticultural (bulb-growing) interests did not develop until the seventeenth century. The fifteenth century, however, witnessed considerable industrial expansion accompanied by a rapid increase of population. Haarlem had 5,000 inhabitants in 1400, 20,000 in 1500 and 40,000 in 1600; these increases resemble in proportion, though not of course in magnitude, those that took place in British towns during the nineteenth century, and they gave rise to planning and housing problems not dissimilar in nature. A great extension was therefore planned about 1426 to take in low-lying peaty ground south and west of the fortification moat; and for the first time the characteristics of a grachtenstad became apparent in the city. The former en-circling moat now acted as an urban waterway; drainage canals were dug to enclose long, shallow building blocks whose surface level was raised by building up with sand from the Spaarne bed; streets and "steegen" were set out; and the whole area was enclosed by new drainage and fortification moats, the Raamsingel and Zijlsingel. The fortified area of the city now totalled some 890 acres. Plan 54 gives little idea of the form that the new development took, for it is a map of a city in ruins: a great fire in 1576 had resulted in widespread damage, and the survey from which this map was drawn was made with the intention of showing the extent of damage in preparation for rebuilding. The redevelopment scheme that followed will be examined in Chapter VII.

Notable changes in the town centre took place as a result of considerable enlargements of St. Bavo church towards the end of the fifteenth century. The vast building (55, 56) now occupied most of the eastern portion of the original open space, thus reducing the extent of the market place and blocking the entrance on to it of several minor streets on the southern side. The celebrated architect, Lieven de Key, commissioned by the City Council to build a Butchers' Hall, took the opportunity of preparing a redevelopment scheme for the market area as a whole. He added a new wing to the town hall, thus completing the western flank of the square, and further reduced the extent of open space by siting a row of buildings immediately west of the church; the one nearest the church was his splendid Vleeshal (1603), with stepped gables, rich ornamentation and shining copper roof, which was among the finest works of architecture in the Netherlands of that time (55). De Key also encouraged rebuilding in mutually sympathetic styles of houses along the northern and eastern flanks. Increase in the general height of buildings, coupled with decrease in the extent of the square, resulted in a better sense of scale in the composition as a whole, whilst reduction in the number of minor streets having direct access to the square and improved façade treatment made for greater

55. *Haarlem: St. Bavokerk and Vleeshal, 1603, from town hall*

continuity and enclosure in a very impressive civic and commercial centre. Its appearance towards the end of the seventeenth century is excellently recalled by the painting of Gerrit Berckheyde (1638–98) in the National Gallery, London.

Haarlem in the late sixteenth century must have presented an impressive silhouette to the

56. *Haarlem: shops adjoining St. Bavokerk on south side*

*57. Haarlem: Amsterdamschepoort,
circa 1450*

*58. Haarlem: terrace, 1612, in
Groot Heiligland*

besieging Spaniards. Its mediaeval fortifications, of moat, brick wall incorporating many half-round towers and nine gates, of which the Amsterdamschepoort (57) is the only survivor, gave a decorative if no longer efficient setting to the great cathedral and the many church spires that rose above them. Early in the following century, when stout efforts were still being made to make good the havoc wrought by Spanish bombardment and the great fire of 1576, many new houses were built. Many hofjes were also restored. One of them, in the Groot Heiligland, now houses the Frans Hals Museum; and on the opposite side of the same street is a terrace of former hofjes characteristic of the unpretentious, urbane domestic street architecture of the day (58).

ALKMAAR ("all sea") shows more clearly than any other Dutch town the contrast between the geestgrond foundation and the grachtenstad extension. It is an ancient settlement; the name first occurs in the tenth century as a fishing village situated in the midst of marshes and lakes, and it is mentioned as a market in 1134. A charter was granted by Count William II of Holland in 1254.

The early mediaeval town occupied a key position in the North Holland Province. It was sited at the eastern end of a sand tongue protruding into clay and marsh near the north-west corner of the large Schermer Lake, whose waters, linked with others, afforded a shipping route to the Zuider Zee ports of Hoorn, Enkhuisen and Medemblik. To the east lay the Voormeer, a shallow part of the Schermer; to the west, a few miles away, were the North Sea dunes but no direct water link between town and sea could be made through them; to the north a dike road had been constructed by the Count of Holland to facilitate communication with West Friesland, and one of the three castles built by him to protect this route was sited at the north-east corner of the town.

59. *Alkmaar: Langestraat, town hall at left and St. Laurenskerk*

The approximate extent of the geest-grond town is indicated on the key to Drebbel's plan (60). Its development was well controlled; the central axis, the long, straight Langestraat (59) connected the Grootekerk and its complex of monastic buildings to the principal quay, the Mient. Minor streets, scarcely more than 12 feet wide, ran parallel with and at right angles to this axis, forming an orderly though not dully uniform series of building blocks. The town hall had its site along the Langestraat and the weighing hall, a building of exceptional architectural merit converted in 1582 from its former use as a chapel, occupied a prominent position on the Mient as one sees in the engraving reproduced (61).

The proximity of the new West Friesland road and the building of the castle gave increased strategic significance to the city and strengthened its market func-tion. Richly productive pasture lands in the vicinity brought great prosperity to dairying, and industries such as brewing, extraction of salt from peat, sail-making and ropemaking added their quota to the communal wealth. When town extension became imperative the only course open to the Council was to reclaim part of the Voormeer and develop it as a grachtenstad. The actual date of the extension is in doubt; in fact the authorities give little guidance on the growth of Alkmaar during the fourteenth and fifteenth centuries; but it was

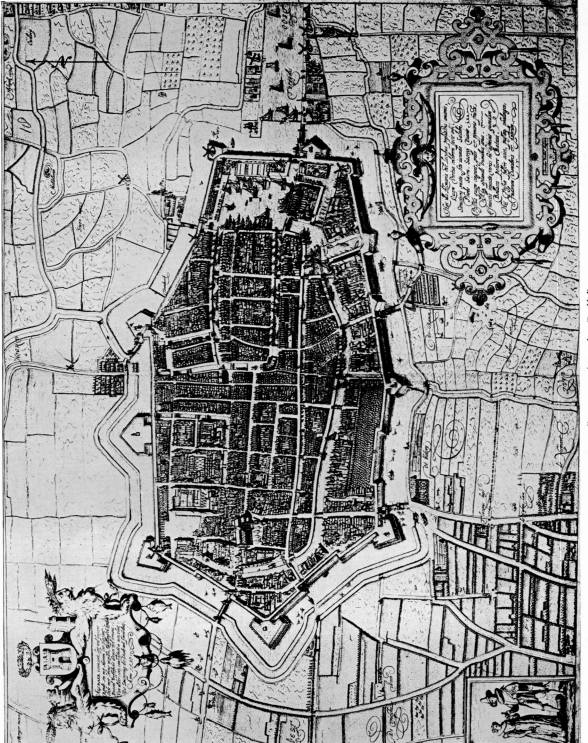

60 *Alkmaar 1597 (Cornelius Drebbel)*

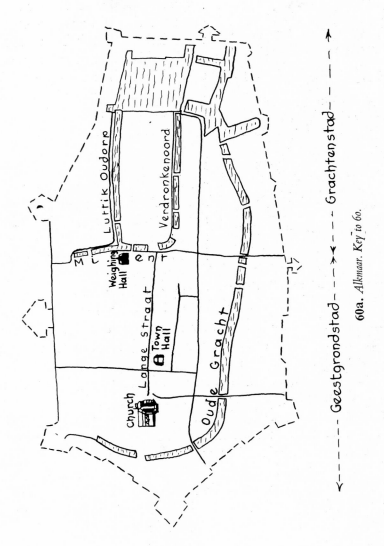

Luttik Oudorp

Verdronkenoord

M

e

n

t

Weighing Hall

Lange Straat

Town Hall

Church

Oude Gracht

‹--- Geestgrondstad ---›--‹--- Grachtenstad ---›

60a. Alkmaar. Key to 60.

61. *Alkmaar: Weighing Hall and Cheese Market (Romeyn de Hooghe, 1675)*

62. *Alkmaar: Luttik Oudorp, "trap-gevel" at right 1609, and Weighing Hall*

certainly completed and the whole area surrounded with wall and moat before 1560, when Jacob van Deventer made survey and drew his map.

That the new town was successfully integrated with the old is demonstrated by the plans. The Oude Gracht changed its function from outer defence canal to principal, inner, lateral waterway, and two broad canal connections were made between the Mient and the new harbour. The more northerly of these, the Luttik Oudorp, was made axial on the weighing hall (62). The two parts of the city are distinct and yet in harmony; the earlier part is seen to be slightly higher (39 shows an approximate comparison of levels) and such place-names as Geeststraat and Hoogstraat identify its origin; whilst if confirmation of the history of the lower part were needed it is supplied by the place-names Verdron kenoord (drowned place), Fnidsen (a corruption of Venice) and Groot- and Klein-Nieuwland. As befits a grachtenstad, the principal means of communication are by water; some of its streets are too narrow for any but pedestrian traffic.

Alkmaar has from earliest times displayed a vitality which enabled it to survive, and indeed to assist in bringing about, extraordinary changes in geographical and economic conditions. It adapted itself with dexterity from the functions required of an inland port surrounded by marsh and lake to those of a market centre surrounded by *polderland*; in 1500 there were still mariners and sea-going ships within its walls; by 1700 it dominated and administered a large agricultural region. But by far the most colourful function which the city still performs, as it has done for centuries past, is that of cheese market for North Holland. White-clad porters of the Cheese Guild, wearing broad-brimmed straw hats of bright red, green, blue or yellow according to which company of the Guild they belong, throng the square beside the great weighing hall on the Mient on Friday mornings, carting high piles of yellow cheeses to be weighed and sold. The scene has changed little since Romeyn de Hooghe portrayed it so vividly on his engraving of 1675 (61).

The grachtensteden serve to show that, to the Dutch, town planning is no modern science. Where the only extension areas available were on land that had to be diligently adapted for building purposes and constantly protected and preserved by skilful manipulation of water levels, town planning and controlled development were indispensable. But strict regulation of development produced no stereotyped plan, no regimentation, no overbuilding to extract the maximum use from the last square yard. The cities here described displayed a remarkable variety in layout; one had a rectangular motif, another a concentric, another a cellular. Yet they were all united by characteristic features, calm, tree-lined canals, some flanked by elegant mansions and others by unassertive dwellings, workshops

63. *Tholen: view from outer side of southernmost bastion*

and warehouses, long rectangular building blocks separated by narrow lanes, strong contrast of scale in the canal thoroughfare and the corridor street, the high-arched stone bridge, the ubiquitous windmill. But above all they shared two features, the dramatic silhouette of tall spires of church, town hall and gate soaring out of the flatness of the landscape, and the pronounced line of demarcation between town and country enforced by the encircling canal. Straggling, ribbon development was, and in general still is, conspicuously absent, and such scenes as illustrated in Tholen (63)—the birthplace, it may be mentioned, of Vermuyden, the drainer of the English fens—were the rule rather than the exception.

REFERENCES

1. NIERMEYER, J. F., *Delft en Delfland, hun oorsprong en vroegste geschiedenis*, 1944, p. 83.
2. FOCKEMA ANDREAE, S. J., *op. cit.*, p. 87.
3. EAST, W. G., *An Historical Geography of Europe*, 1950, p. 253.
4. VAN OERLE, H., *Oud Leiden*, 1943, p. 9, and others.
5. See also GRASWINCKEL, D. P. M., *Nederlandsche Hofjes*, 1943, a study of charitable foundations of this type in 28 Dutch towns.
6. See engraving by C. J. VISSCHER, 1623, in PETERS, C. H., *op. cit.*, Vol. II, p. 337.
7. PETERS, C. H., *op. cit.*, Vol. I, p. 251.

CHAPTER V

Mediaeval Town Foundation
and Development: IV

High-ground Towns

FAMILIAR among the mediaeval towns of Europe are those typified by Durham, Carcassonne Cité, Rothenburg, Segovia and Caltanisetta, to name but a few, which cling to and appear almost to grow out of a hill site. The Netherlands can show no such examples, for the only hills worthy of the name occur in districts which have never been conducive to urban habitation. It has, never-theless, many old towns built upon gently sloping sites well above flood level whose layouts do not reveal the unmistakable national characteristics noted in previous chapters but resemble those of contemporary towns in other European countries.

Such towns fall within the "chance-grown" category; they appear to have developed with little constraint and with scant evidence of an overall plan. The site configuration is to a large extent reflected in the street pattern and in the placing of buildings. The streets tend, like Corbusier's pack donkey, to follow the easiest route that the ground presented; they are not straight for any appre-ciable distance and seldom cross each other at right angles; slight changes in direction and occasional variations in the building line produce interesting contrasts of lateral space and a constantly changing street picture. Building blocks resulting from a somewhat haphazard road pattern are of irregular shape, and tend to be of greater length than depth so as to make maximum use of main street frontage. Waterways, if present, do not dominate the scene.

It generally happens that Dutch high-ground towns have at least one central space, acting as market place and civic centre, the arrangement and appearance of which are typical of mediaeval towns elsewhere in Europe. In shape it is rarely a regular geometrical figure; at Middelburg, for instance, it is an irregular pen-tagon, at Breda an elongated quadrilateral and at Oldenzaal approximately trapezoidal. Its façade is not noticeably interrupted by streets debouching into the space, partly because their width in comparison with the length or breadth of the market place is very small and partly because they mostly approached it on a slightly curved alignment. The same sense of enclosure in the space is as evident in Dutch towns of this type as, for example, in the Grand' Place of Brussels, the Place Verte of Antwerp, the Mercato Vecchio of Siena or the Marktplatz of Nuremberg.

The only component of which the construction was necessarily the subject of a premeditated decision was the defence wall, with its gates and encircling moat. The paramount importance of protection in mediaeval times made the provision of adequate fortification a primary duty of town councils and, moreover, a town could rarely qualify for a charter unless it was walled. Defences were therefore planned with considerable care and, the shortest perimeter for a given area being a circle, the line of the wall, which tended also to conform with the slopes of the terrain, was rounded rather than square. Middelburg, Breda, Oldenzaal, Zwolle and Amersfoort were all approximately circular in outline. The practice of leaving gates which formerly belonged to inner walls as decorative features within an extended town is as familiar in Dutch cities as elsewhere; the Plompetoren of Amersfoort, like the Markusturm of Rothenburg, served for many years as town gaol; inner gates still survive in old cities of Europe, notably the Porte de Hal of Brussels, and even the gates of London were standing until well into the eighteenth century.

AMERSFOORT ("fort on the Amer") affords a good illustration of the high-ground town. It originated upon an elevated, sandy site, skirted on the western flank by a river formerly called the Eem but now known as the Amer. An ancient overland route from Utrecht to Deventer crossed the river at a fordable point and the ford received the protection of a castle built probably during the tenth century. No evidence exists as to the precise location of the castle but it is thought to have occupied the site of the present market place. Although the name Amersfoort occurs in documents as early as 1028,[1] it was not until 1259 that the settlement had attained sufficient importance to merit a charter; this was granted by the Bishop of Utrecht who wished to make it a fortress in the defence system against attack from Gelderland.

The first wall and moat, constructed between the years 1228 and 1259, enclosed an area of some forty acres (see Braun and Hogenberg's plan, 64). Of the four gates included in this wall two survive, the Kamperbinnenpoort and the Plompetorenpoort (65, 66). The market place developed on what were probably the

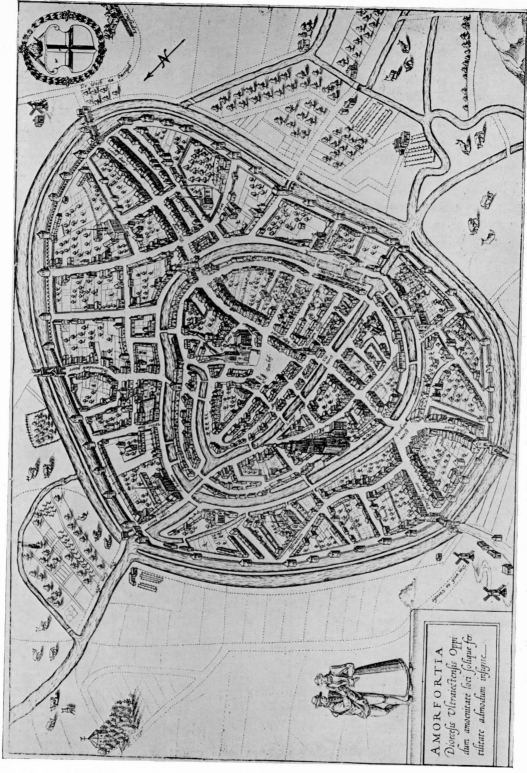

64. *Amersfoort, circa 1580 (Braun and Hogenberg)*

65. *Amersfoort: Kamperbinnenpoort, circa 1400, O.L.V. Tower at left*

66. *Amersfoort: Secretarishuisje, circa 1600, and Plompetorenpoort, circa 1300*

grounds of the castle. The building of St. Joriskerk (67) on its northern flank started in 1247, though its present form dates from 1534, and the town hall stood on the western flank, as shown on the plan. Demolition of the latter in 1759 left a void in a market place which was already too large architecturally; even now the surrounding buildings, with the exception of the church, have insufficient height in proportion to the length and breadth of the space and the whole composition is rather out of scale.

Prosperity came to the city during the thirteenth and fourteenth centuries. Apart from its role of fortress and its flourishing brewing industry it had three other functions: it was a link in the road traffic system between the eastern hinterland and Utrecht and later, Amsterdam; a river port with a small harbour and wharfage area north-west of the market place; and a market centre for the surrounding villages. Farmers in the vicinity were obliged to send their grain to be ground in the town's windmills, a cluster of which are seen from old maps to have stood outside the Utrecht gate to the south-west. As wealth and influence

increased, the space within the walls became fully
utilized and straggling
"suburban" growth, in-
cluding several monastic
foundations, began to
spread over the open land
immediately outside. To
provide the necessary protection for these suburbs,
as well as defended living
and working space for the
expanding population, a

67. *Amersfoort: St. Joriskerk and market place, from O.L.V. Tower*

second circumferential wall was commenced in 1381.

It was not completed until 1450. The digging of the broad moat and the
construction of the wall proved to be an immense task. Nearly two miles in
length, it had thirty-nine watch towers and seven gates, including the fine watergate at the north-west corner, the Koppelpoort astride the river Amer (68). The
undertaking imposed a severe strain upon the resources of the city, so much so
that fines and other penalties were ordered to be paid in bricks; it is recorded that
the neighbouring town of Baarn pledged itself in 1443 to provide and maintain
in perpetuity 120 metres of wall.[2] To obtain further funds the Council sold the
land made available by the demolition of the inner wall in lots for building
purposes, and this transaction fortunately achieved something more than the

68. *Amersfoort: Koppelpoort water gate, circa 1400*

mere provision of extra
revenue for a depleted trea-
sury: it enabled the building of the *muurhuisen*, the
wall-houses, for which
Amersfoort is unique in
the Netherlands. These
simple, substantial and often individually attractive
buildings lining a gently
curving street are a very
distinctive feature of the
old city (*66, 69, 70*).

69. *Amersfoort: wall houses north-eastwards from O.L.V. Tower*

The plan of about 1580 (*64*) shows that the space made available by this great extension was by no means fully utilized a century afterwards; nor do maps of the seventeenth century show much closer development. This was because the rate of the city's economic progress was slowed up during the sixteenth and seventeenth centuries; the wave of prosperity that swept through the water towns of Holland during the "Golden Age" did not reach as far as Amersfoort. Thus it is that, apart from the magnificent Ons Lieve Vrouwe Toren, the Gothic church tower (1471) rising to a commanding height of 312 feet, the city can display few buildings of a monumental nature. Its principal attractions lie in the harmonious grouping of its buildings rather than their individual qualities, in the curves and minor deviations in its streets and building lines and the variety of vistas which they present, in the unexpected little "places" formed where roads or footpaths meet (*70*) and in the general absence of formality of layout. It evinces much of the "accidental" beauty that Camillo Sitte[3] admired in the chance-grown mediaeval town.

ZUTPHEN came into being on a low, rounded hill at the confluence of two rivers, the wide trade highway of the Ijssel and the minor Berkel. It consists of three parts, an informal early mediaeval nucleus, an extension of bastide character, and another extension which grew so haphazardly that it can scarcely be said to have any form at all.

70. *Amersfoort: "Het Sluisje", wall house with tower from the fourteenth-century fortifications*

99

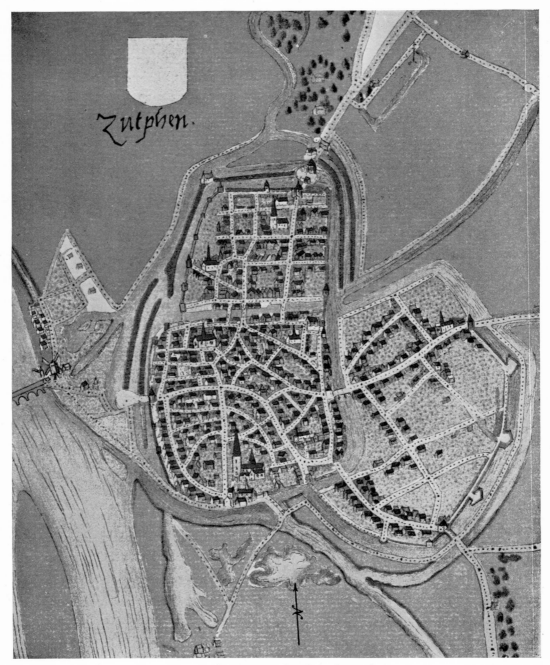

71. *Zutphen, circa 1570 (Jacob van Deventer)*

The first settlement may well have existed in Frankish times, although the first recorded reference to it as an "oppidum" is dated 1095. It is considered likely[4] that a pre-town burcht settlement occupied the summit of the hill, around the base of which were later sited the three town markets. No vestige of such a kernel survives, however, and the town to which a charter was granted in 1190 was approximately rectangular in shape, some 35 acres in area, and bounded by the Berkel on the west and north and by a canal on the east and south connecting to the Ijssel (see van Deventer's map, 71). Its salient feature was a broad street starting at the western, Ijssel, gate, rising gradually through the vegetable market to the wood market, and thence curving gently downhill through the seed market to the south-eastern gate (now the Drogenapstoren). Another street of lesser importance—its width is somewhat exaggerated on plan 71—led from the town centre to the southern gate near which were the Gravenhof, a residence of the Counts of Gelderland, and the twelfth-century church of St. Walburg, standing in usual Dutch tradition away from the scene of daily activity in a small enclosure of its own. Other streets were narrow and followed the contours, and the pattern they produced was so lacking in formality that no two building blocks were of the same shape.

As has already been mentioned,[5] the situation of Zutphen was sufficiently favourable in relation to the ancient and thriving capital of Overijssel, Deventer, to lead the Count of Gelderland to foster its development as a rival. He caused an extension to be made on firm ground north of the Berkel towards the end of the thirteenth century; its layout, apart from a certain eccentricity on the western side due to the ground slopes, resembles that of the bastides described in Chapter III. The new town at first enjoyed independence of the old city, and had its own church and market place as well as status as a separate port with individual access to the Ijssel; but it was brought under the control of the City Council when a defence wall surrounding both settlements was completed in 1312. Incorporated in this wall was a fine water gate, now in ruin, spanning the Berkel at the south-west corner of the new town; it is curious that Jacob van Deventer did not show this on his plan of 1570 though it is to be seen on that of Pontanus (72).

The second extension, made to the east of the old city about 1450, had as its primary object the protection of a hospital and a certain amount of suburban sprawl that had taken place there. From the first, little control seems to have been exercised over development in this area. Plan 71 shows only scattered growth and from plan 72, dated 1639, the built-up area is seen to have been reduced: this was because a number of buildings both there and in the old city

72. *Zutphen, 1639 (J. Pontanus)*

had to be demolished to make way for much more extensive and powerful fortifications made necessary by improved technique in artillery during the fifteenth, sixteenth and seventeenth centuries, a subject that will be referred to in the next chapter.

The three parts of Zutphen have never merged into a successful unity; they still stand apart both in the physical sense and in the characteristics which they display. The old centre has beauty and vitality: the broad, well-proportioned seed market is terminated very pleasantly by a fine late Gothic four-storey house in brick (Zaadmarkt 109, dated 1549) and, behind it, the soaring Drogenap-storen, seen in photograph 73 from outside the southern boundary; the graceful curve of the wood market leads up to the central crossroads where the tall and elegant

73. *Zutphen: Drogenapstoren, 1465*

Wijnhuis stands; and the vegetable market, with the Wijnhuis as its northern closing feature and, formerly, a town gate at its southern end, is the third distinct yet accordant element of the principal commercial area. Van Deventer's plan fails to show the spatial contrasts in these three markets and Pontanus gives insufficient emphasis to the proportions of the seed market. By contrast, the *Nieuwstad* is rather dull in appearance whilst the aimless eastern extension patently betrays its origin as a mere appendage having no organic connection with the other parts.

The plan of the town of DEVENTER (74) is included here to illustrate a type of fortification rather than a town layout form but some features characteristic of the "chance-grown" town may be observed from it. The large, irregularly shaped market place, entered from the quay at the south-eastern corner through a city gate, is flanked by shops, office-and-warehouse buildings and craftsmen's houses, and has as an imposing, central feature, standing in isolation, the very tall and picturesque weighing hall built in 1528. At its northern end the place widens out into proportions which are somewhat unmanageable architecturally, and the sense of enclosure usually associated with the mediaeval town square is in conse-quence lost. The hill, called with some overstatement "Het Berg", which over-

74. *Deventer, 1648 (Joannes Blaeu)*

looks the northern end, is capped with a twelfth-century church but the cathedral is sited near the bridge over the Ijssel. The town hall stands immediately to the east of the cathedral. The pattern of streets and building blocks is very reminiscent of the casual growth of the mediaeval high-ground town.

REFERENCES

1. VAN HASSELT, J. F. B., *Amersfoort rondom zijn Toren*, 1948, p. 27.
2. VAN BEMMEL, A., *Beschrijving der Stad Amersfoort*, 1750, p. 20.
3. SITTE, CAMILLO, *L'Art de Bâtir les Villes*, 1889.
4. FOCKEMA ANDREAE, S. J., *op. cit.*, p. 70.
5. *Supra*, p. 29.

CHAPTER VI

Background to Development

Fourteenth to Seventeenth Centuries

THE EMERGENCE OF A NATION

TOWARDS the end of the fourteenth century the vagaries of dynastic succession brought about for the first time some semblance of political unification in the Low Countries, when they came under the rule of the House of Burgundy. By the middle of the following century the Netherlands provinces formed part of a large buffer state extending between France and Germany and embracing Flanders, Hainault and Luxemburg. The unification went only as far as acceptance by each province of Burgundian sovereignty and of a provincial governor, a Stadhouder or Lieutenant, appointed by the Duke. At all levels of government the traditional love of independence was strongly in evidence: provinces retained their entity as administrative units and stubbornly resisted any attempts to establish a centralized government; the provinces, acting together as the States Assembly, remained sufficiently powerful to withhold support for political or military measures taken by the Duke without first seeking their consent; and town councils insisted upon the observance by higher authority of their rights as set out in hard-won charters, which had already proved their worth over previous centuries.

Another dynastic accident at the beginning of the sixteenth century caused the Burgundian inheritance to be united with Spain, and the Netherlands thus became part of the mightiest empire of Europe. In the first stages of the new order no very noticeable change occurred in the social and political structure of the States, but gradually the Emperor Charles V and his less tactful successor Philip II imposed increasingly heavy taxation and tried to usurp ancient privileges. Occupation by a foreign army and attempts to stamp out the Protestant faith, which had made substantial headway in the northern provinces especially, led to strong resentment of Spanish rule, and an undercurrent of rebellion stirred among the towns and provinces. In 1567 Philip sent the Duke of Alva to act as

106

Governor and quell what in the first instance was a bout of religious rioting, but the ferocity with which he subdued the anti-Catholic rioters and the cruelty and violence of his methods of government precipitated the revolt of the United Netherlands and the beginning of the Eighty Years War. The struggle for territorial and municipal independence had thus become identified with a national resistance movement in which political and economic motives were united with religious convictions against a foreign tyranny.

The revolt was led, at first somewhat unwillingly, by the great statesman and patriot, William ("the Silent"), Prince of Orange, who had earlier been appointed by Philip as Stadhouder of Holland, Zeeland, Friesland and Utrecht. His small and ill-equipped army of ducal retainers and foreign mercenaries was a poor match against the professional might of Spain. On the seas his "water-beggars" harassed Spanish supply ships and warships and assisted in the relief of ports. On land the uneven struggle was largely a battle of towns. The inhabitants of Naarden and Zutphen were slaughtered almost to a man; Haarlem and Zieriksee withstood siege for many months before capitulation; Alkmaar and Leiden, besieged to the point of starvation, drove the enemy from their gates by opening dikes to flood the precious surrounding countryside. For sixteen years the Prince of Orange carried the burden of directing and financing the war, as well as seeking foreign aid and presenting the justice of his country's case to the rulers of Europe. His steadfast leadership sustained the tired citizen armies, rallied the murmurers and waverers and eventually welded a country of individualists into a proud nation. The Prince did not live to see the fulfilment of his life's work for he fell to an assassin's bullet at Delft in 1584; but the struggle persisted, with later distinguished contributions in leadership from his two sons and his grandson, until the seven northern provinces finally established their independence from Spain in 1609 although the Dutch Republic was not formally proclaimed until 1648.

ECONOMIC ASCENDANCY

Whether a Burgundian duke or a Spanish emperor held sovereignty over the Netherlands, it made little difference to the merchant. He complied with ducal or royal foreign policy if it suited him; if high policy made the country of his customers an enemy he regarded the customer as more important than the policy; his actions were in no way motivated or fettered by patriotic sentiments, for until the death of William the Silent patriotism was a thing practically unknown in the Netherlands.

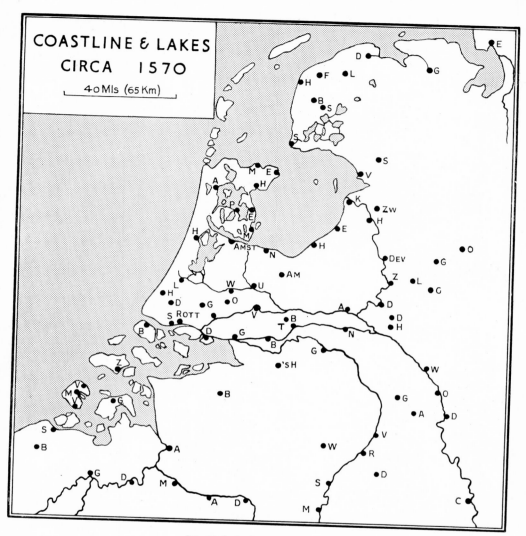

COASTLINE & LAKES CIRCA 1570

40 Mls (65 Km)

75. *Netherlands, 1579-1609*

Throughout the thirteenth and fourteenth centuries Dutch sailors, ably directed by Dutch merchants, pursued trade relentlessly wherever they could find it. Towards the end of the fourteenth century they challenged the almost supreme power of the Hanseatic League, and by the end of the following century they had overcome it. Dutch ships were well known in most ports of northern Europe, carrying furs from Russia, wheat from Poland, cloth from Flanders. A vast

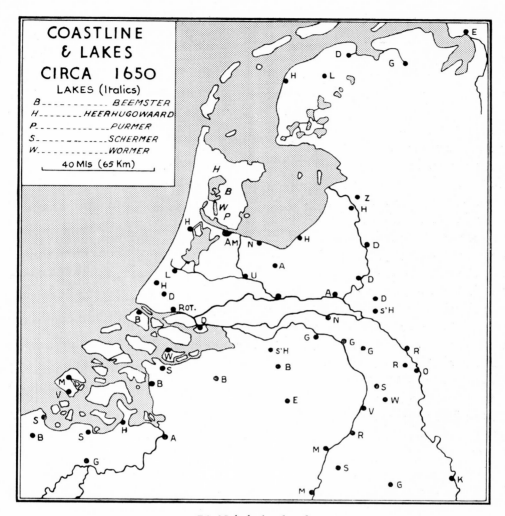

76. *Netherlands, 1609-48*

export in salted herrings had been built up, Dutch beer was in great demand and home-produced cloth, especially the coarser variety made in Haarlem and Leiden, found ready markets in Baltic countries. The ever-growing carrying fleet demanded and encouraged shipbuilding, sailmaking, ropemaking and similar industries. Dannett, translating Guicciardini in 1593, gave this account of the economic activities of the Dutch people: "They are skilful in merchandise and excel in all the arts, namely making of woollen, tapistrey, wusteds, ruffels, linnen, fustian, and other merchandises, and small mercery wares of all sorts and prices which are sent to the whole world. Now also they make silks and wrought velvets after the manner of the people of the Levant . . . they taught Englishmen the art of making woollen cloathes, and of diying, about the year of Our Lord 1404 who till that time were utterlie ignorant thereof. . . ."[1]

Upon the fall of Antwerp to the Spaniards and its near-destruction in 1568 Amsterdam, whose citizens had kept out of the war until it suited them to join in, seized the initiative and rapidly developed as the financial centre for the Low Countries and secured a leading place among the commercial cities of Europe. The policy of religious toleration, inspired and championed by William the Silent, brought thousands of refugees from various parts of Europe, Portuguese Jews, French and Flemish weavers particularly, to add their capital and skill to the national economy. The Jews settled mostly in Amsterdam; the weavers found employment in Haarlem and Leiden, and some of them made valuable contributions to the specialist silk and velvet industries of Amsterdam and Utrecht respectively.

In the first decades of the seventeenth century the Netherlands had emerged as the greatest seafaring nation of Europe with the largest merchant fleet in the world. Sir Walter Raleigh is said to have informed Queen Elizabeth in 1600 that the British had 300 ships in their Baltic fleet whereas the Dutch had 3,000; and a French statesman in 1650 complained that of the 25,000 ships that carried the trade of Europe 14,000 to 15,000 belonged to Holland but only 600 to France.[2] The East India Company, established in 1602, opened up vast new sources of wealth. Dutch sailors were to be found in all parts of the globe; they discovered Tasmania and New Zealand and were the first Europeans to trade with the Japanese. It is a remarkable accomplishment of this small country, not much larger than Wales, that it founded future capital cities in three continents, Batavia (1619), New Amsterdam (1625) and Capetown (1652). The "Golden Age" of unparalleled prosperity, achieved by astonishing enterprise and drive though not without ruthless exploitation and slavery in distant countries and sweated labour at home, lasted until Britain arose to challenge it and gain commercial supremacy in the eighteenth century.

LAND RECLAMATION

The work of protecting land against flooding by sea, river and lake (see map 75), which had started on a small scale during the eighth century, received many setbacks during the two succeeding centuries as a result of inefficient diking

techniques coupled with abnormally high tides. By the eleventh century techniques had been improved, and the Middle Ages saw a steady increase in the
area of land reclaimed. Water Catchment Boards, independent public authorities charged with the duty of reclaiming, maintaining and administering new
lands, were set up early in the thirteenth century and many still function.

Each province presented its own peculiar physical problems. In Zeeland the
major task was the building of heavy sea dikes to protect existing land and to
make fresh land available by joining islands together. It was an arduous task
demanding prodigious patience and fortitude. Some islands actually shifted their
positions, for whilst land was being reclaimed at one end the sea would wash
away part of the other: this occurred at one time in the island of South Beveland.

In Holland proper, where the sea dunes held firmly but the level of the land
itself was constantly sinking, the two essentials were to hold rivers to their courses
and to prevent the spread of inland lakes, most of which were linked to the
Zuider Zee. The Rhine and its various tributaries were banked with high
dikes and, over the centuries, their waters were made to flow in shorter and
more convenient channels, the routes of which received frequent revision. The
lakes were sometimes enlarged by fierce storms and high winds, but often their
spreading resulted from the actions of men: as Holland and Friesland had always
lacked forest very little wood was available for fuel and peat was in great demand;
each town or village had its own lake from which supplies could be obtained,
and the greater the amount removed the greater became the extent of the lake.
A whole series of precisely rectangular basins with this origin fringe, for instance,
the Loosdrecht lakes between Amsterdam and Utrecht. An added incentive
for peat-digging was that its ashes contained salt which, when refined, was a
valuable export commodity and an essential factor in the herring industry. In
course of time extensive exploitation caused the inundation of much land, and
the pressure of water weakening the dikes in the vicinity sometimes resulted in the
disappearance of entire villages. Amsterdam itself was once threatened by the
expansion of the largest lake of all, the Haarlemmermeer. Since the sixteenth
century, therefore, official consent was given to promoters of large-scale peat-
winning operations only if they undertook to reclaim the lakes so formed.

The first step in the reclamation of great lakes was to isolate them from the
open sea, with which most of them were connected by narrow inlets. From the
thirteenth century onwards dams were built across these inlets: the Schardam in
1315 isolated the great Beemster lake and the Monnikendam, 1401, the Purmer
lake. The seaward side of the dam was then available for storage purposes and

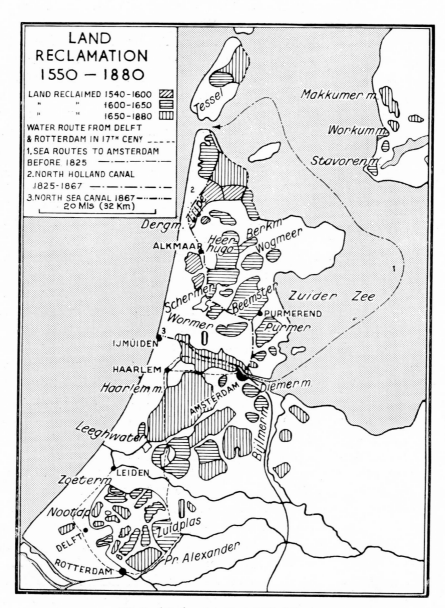

77. *Land Reclamation, North Holland Province*

the level of water on the land side could be controlled by pumping surplus water over the dam into storage basins or *boezems* at low tide. The benefits of such dams were that high dikes were not needed to keep lakes within bounds and that salt water could no longer penetrate far into the country; lake waters became fresh within a few years of damming and the land which eventually replaced them could be rendered fertile in a much shorter period.

Individual "polders", the name given to reclaimed lands, were separated from each other by dikes and intersected by ditches providing for surface water drainage. Within a polder, therefore, water could be controlled and any surplus discharged into storage basins. For polders situated near the sea, polder water was connected to the outer water by means of sluices which opened at low tide to enable the inner water to flow away, and for those at some distance from sea or tidal river a canal system of drainage had to be used. According to Dibbits[3] wind watermills were brought into use as early as the thirteenth century for pumping water from polder to *boezem*, but it was not until the fifteenth century that their employment for this purpose became general practice.

The size and shape of the country continued to vary during the late Middle Ages. Water driven away from one area would often return to engulf another. The great disaster of 1421 has already been referred to: the failure of the Meuse dikes caused the flooding of a large polder and the formation of a vast inlet south of Dordrecht (cf. maps 4 and 5). Further major inundations in various parts of the country were recorded in 1508, 1509, 1514, 1516 and 1532. Despite these losses, however, astonishingly rapid progress was made in stemming the floods and regaining large tracts of land. William the Silent gave ardent encouragement to the work, and during the "Golden Age" wealthy merchants saw it as a very profitable field of investment for the capital accruing from overseas trade. In the period 1590–1640 some 200,000 acres were added to the Netherlands, and over the next century another 110,000 acres followed[4] (compare maps 75, 76). Geographers must have been very much occupied in keeping the national map up to date.

The skilled and patient work of two celebrated "landmakers", Andries Vierlingh (1507–80) and Jan Leeghwater (1575–1650), contributed much to this remarkable achievement. Vierlingh, a specialist in diking, concentrated on preserving and shortening the coastline and keeping the great rivers under control. Leeghwater was the first to make large-scale use of the wind watermill for pumping water out of polders. Map 77 gives an indication of the chief areas reclaimed in North Holland Province during the years 1540–1650. The Zijpe was won from the sea in 1599 and the remainder from lakes of about seven feet in depth: the Wogmeer in 1608, the Beemster in 1612, Purmer 1622, Wormer 1626, Heer Hugoward 1631 and Schermer 1635. The largest, the Beemster, was nearly 18,000 acres in extent and the Schermer with its fourteen separate polders yielded more than 12,000 acres. By 1640 Leeghwater had to his credit the reclamation of 27 lakes in the region north of Amsterdam. His ambition was to drain the vast Haarlemmermeer (45,000 acres) and he planned to use 160 windmills for the operation; but it was not until 1852, and after fifteen successive schemes had been considered, that this mighty feat was eventually accomplished. Leeghwater's fame was such that his advice was requested upon drainage and reclamation work in England, France, Germany and Denmark. Yet, as Vlekke writes,[5] "he remained a simple working man, the master mechanic and carpenter who, in between the draining of swamps, devoted his time to the construction of clocks for church towers, and felt honoured when he was allowed to wait upon His Excellency, the Prince of Orange, and the city aristocrats who had come to 'open' the newly reclaimed polder in the Beemster." His versatility also embraced the architectural sphere: the gable designs of his *Raadhuisjes*, the equivalent in villages of a town hall, in the North Holland region are delightful and unique; that at De Rijp is particularly pleasing.

Although North Holland Province was the scene of more spectacular achievements in reclamation steady progress was also made elsewhere in the country, notably in the south-western region, as comparison of maps 75 and 76 indicates. Large marshy tracts west and south-west of Dordrecht were turned into spacious polders; the Zeeland islands were gradually pieced together; and the island of Goeree-Overflakkee, barely 10,000 acres in extent before the fifteenth century, was increased fourfold during that century and received some 15,000 additional acres by the end of the sixteenth century. The new land varied in quality. Where the water table was fairly low, as in parts of North Holland and Zeeland, well-drained fertile clay soils yielded abundant grain crops and flax; on lighter soils, as in the vicinity of Leiden, horticulture and market gardening proved very successful; and high water table areas, as Friesland, produced rich meadows. The bold and farsighted policy of wresting land from water proved to be fully justified, and rewarded its promoters with very substantial profits.

TOWN FORTIFICATION. The techniques of warfare had been transformed during the fifteenth and sixteenth centuries by the use of gunpowder and by substantial progress in the effectiveness and destructive power of artillery equipment; and in consequence it became necessary to introduce entirely new methods of town defence. In the Netherlands the war against the Spaniards caused urgent action to be taken in this respect. Tall mediaeval walls of brick proved no match for the new weapons and could be breached without difficulty by the iron cannon ball. To command a sufficiently distant horizon in flat terrain high walls were more than ever necessary, but they required the protection of the *glacis,* the gentle outward slope from the counterscarp. Bastions and ravelins, upon which cannons could be mounted and from which enfilade fire could be brought to bear upon attacking forces, had also to be incorporated into the fortification system. Lavedan refers[6] to the many treatises published by Italian, French and German military engineers and theorists during the sixteenth and early seventeenth centuries, but he makes no mention of the important work in this field of the Dutch engineer Simon Stevin (1548–1620) and only passing reference to the "Dutch Vauban", Menno van Coehorn (1641–1704).

In his *Sterctenbouwing*, published in 1594, Stevin analysed some of the treatises of foreign experts and attempted to adapt the techniques they advocated to the special conditions of his own country. From the defence aspect, he con⁄ sidered the most advantageous shape for a town to be hexagonal with a bastion at each angle. He was, however, less concerned with the presentation of ideal solutions than with the more urgent problem of designing fortifications for existing towns, and accordingly put forward a series of practical suggestions for the most effective design of walls, bastions and canals. These formed the basis of what later came to be known as the "Old Netherlands" defence system, and were implemented in many towns by his contemporary Adriaen Anthonisz. During the period 1570–1600 there was scarcely a town in the Netherlands in which the first improved fortifications were not influenced by him. The features of the system are well illustrated in the maps of Leiden, Alkmaar, Zutphen, Deventer and Willemstad (*46, 60, 72, 74* and *78*). Jacob van Deventer's map of Zutphen (*71*) shows mediaeval walls, gates and watch towers, but the map drawn by Pontanus some seventy years later (plan *72* dated 1639) shows a much wider moat with small bastions and ravelins spaced at rather infrequent intervals around the perimeter. The outer circumferential roads indicated on the former plan are seen to have been eliminated on the latter.

Towards the end of the seventeenth century, when artillery as a weapon of attack had become more efficacious especially as regards range of fire and weight of projectile, further modifications in design for defence had to be made. Menno van Coehorn was the prime mover in introducing them. He published a treatise[7] on the special problems of fortification of towns situated on marshy or low⁄

lying ground in which, *inter alia*, means were suggested whereby the water table of the surrounding terrain could be raised in order to deny an enemy the opportunity of digging-in. The principal improvements introduced by him were enlargement of bastions and ravelins and setting them out at more frequent intervals along the perimeter, provision of gun emplacements at differing levels, camouflage of gun positions and provision of protected routes to armories and magazines. Among examples illustrating his methods, which came to be called the "New Netherlands" system, were the fortifications of Amsterdam (*98*), Bergen-op-Zoom, Doesburg and Nijmegen.

These immense and intricate constructions proved to be so expensive that their installation was permitted only in certain towns selected as key points in the national defence pattern. They occupied a vast area of land—inspection of plans shows that the space devoted to them was often well in excess of the built-up area of the town itself—and they formed an indisputable barrier to casual lateral expansion. In planning a town extension, therefore, the precaution had to be taken to provide a generous area of open space within the new defence perimeter for possible future development. Such an area could prove useful, as has been noted earlier, for grazing cattle in the event of siege; and it also made alternative accommodation available for straggling development outside the walls which was promptly removed by town councils if it interfered with arcs of fire or afforded cover to an attacker. It is of interest that up to the middle of the nineteenth century, long after the need for such forms of fortification had passed, towns still had sufficient land within their walls to accommodate normal increases of population. When walls, bastions and ravelins were eventually demolished their sites were planted to serve as amenities; and thus it is that even until recent times so many Dutch cities had such a pronounced and pleasant "urban fence".

REFERENCES

1. GUICCIARDINI, L., *op. cit.*, p. 15.
2. VAN VEEN, J., *op. cit.*, p. 60.
3. DIBBITS, H. A. M. C., *Nederland-Waterland*, 1950, p. 58.
4. COOLS, R. H. A., *Strijd om den Grond in het lage Nederland*, 1948, p. 131.
5. VLEKKE, B. H. M., *op. cit.*, p. 179.
6. LAVEDAN, P., *Histoire de l'Urbanisme, Renaissance et Temps modernes*, 1941, p. 17.
7. VAN COEHOORN, M., *Nieuwe Vestingbouw op en natte of lage horizont*, 1685. See also SCHUKKING, W. H., *De Oude Vestingwerken van Nederland*, Amsterdam, 1947.

CHAPTER VII

The Renaissance and Dutch Town Planning

THE Renaissance, the emergence of the modern order from the mediaeval, brought to Netherlands towns none of the sudden and dramatic transformations in appearance and layout that were characteristic of urban development elsewhere in Europe during the period. The rapid transition from the institutions and traditions of the Middle Ages to bold new ideas in literature, art, science, politics and religion was accompanied, first in Italy and then in France, by entirely new trends in architecture and civic design; in towns of the Netherlands, however, the reaction to these trends was slow and the change gradual.

It would be over-simplification to explain this by saying that the Netherlanders had never been subject to the brilliant dictatorship of a *roi soleil* but the fact is not without significance. Since the eleventh century they had been a hardworking freedom-loving people, inured to the constant struggle to maintain a livelihood against the harsh conditions imposed by nature and not much exposed to foreign interference by reason of the comparative inaccessibility of their land from the rest of Europe. Their local rulers, on the whole, adopted the attitude not of the petty despot but of the shrewd administrator; their towns were centres of commercial and industrial activity, not monuments to the vanity of a dictator. H. A. L. Fisher[1] wrote of Flemish artists: "Quietly, insensibly, they glided out of the mediaeval into the modern world"; and the phrase aptly describes the development of Dutch towns during this era, with the exception that, as observed in the previous chapter, the system of town fortification underwent drastic alteration: the shell was abruptly modernized, the content only gradually.

Although much has been written of the Renaissance in town planning experienced by Italy, France and Germany, the influence of the movement in the Netherlands appears to have received little attention from English and French town planning historians. The explanation may lie in the fact that

78. *Willemstad, 1632 (M. Boxhoorn)*

Dutch cities do not, in general, exhibit features of such spectacular and monumental character as do some cities in Europe. The work of Dutch planners
does not seem to have been much influenced by the spate of ideas that poured
forth from Italy in the form of architectural treatises, geometrical plans for ideal
cities and new towns, plans for long straight processional streets and impressive
terminating features, plans for set-piece treatment of squares and grandiose
grouping of buildings; it includes none of the essays in conspicuous extravagance
like the Rome of Bernini or the Versailles of Louis XIV, and few of the ducal
ostentations like Charleville or Nancy, Mannheim or Karlsruhe.

This is not to say that the new order of civic design as practised so enthusi-
astically in the rest of Europe was ignored in the Netherlands: on the contrary
the first radial-concentric town, the much quoted Palmanova, had its counterpart
in Coeworden built only four years later (1597); the ducal showpieces of Charleville and Henrichemont were preceded by a quarter of a century by the new
towns of Willemstad and Klundert. But these three towns, and a few polder
villages of which Borselen (built 1616) in South Beveland is a good example,[2]
are all that the Netherlands has to show in the way of Renaissance town foundation.

WILLEMSTAD (78) was designed in 1565 as a village to serve the large
Ruigenhilsche polder (reclaimed three years previously) from which it gained
its first name Ruigenhil. It occupied a site of strategic importance commanding
the point where the wide Hollandse Diep divided into two branches. By order
of William the Silent it was transformed into a fortress town in 1583, and its
"Old Netherlands" fortifications, which enclosed an area of some fifty acres,
included seven bastions representing the seven united provinces of the Netherlands. A broad dike separating the polderland from the Hollandse Diep carried
a road which formed the most northerly street of the town, and was widened
out to form a town square having the dual function of parade ground and
market place. A small harbour adjoined the northern flank of the square and
was connected to the Hollandse Diep via a channel controlled by a sluice.
Building frontages facing the harbour were allotted mainly to office and warehouse use, commercial and military. The town hall was placed on a corner
site just below the dike street, and thence the principal street, a very modest
counterpart of the typical Renaissance avenue, some 700 feet long and 75 feet
wide and regularly planted with trees, led down to the church which stood in
its own little square. These features are illustrated in photograph 79, taken from
the north wall. Two minor canal streets parallel with the principal axis met the

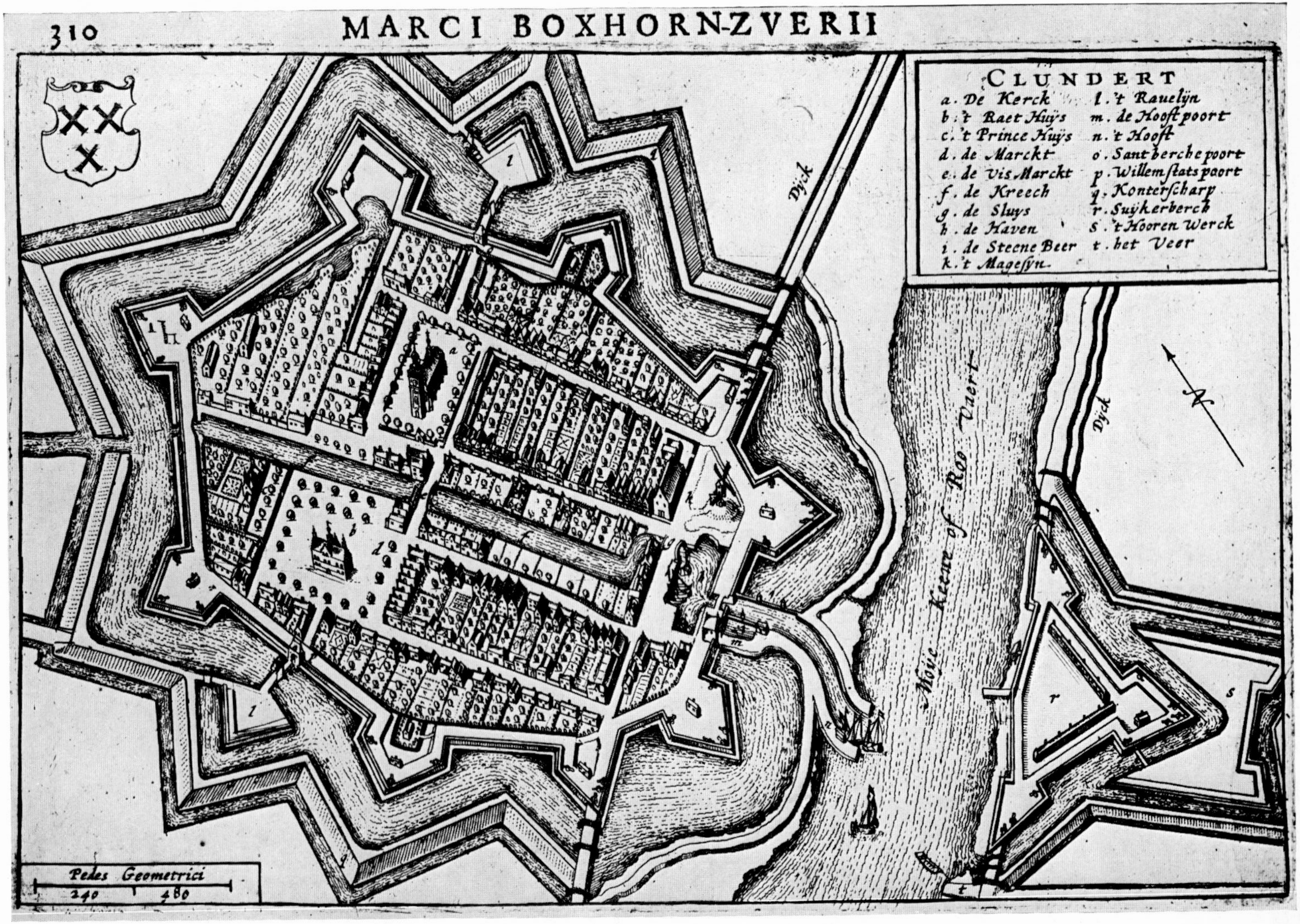

310
MARCI BOXHORN-ZVERII
CLUNDERT
a. De Kerck
b. 't Raet Huÿs
c. 't Prince Huÿs
d. de Marckt
e. de Vis Marckt
f. de Kreech
g. de Sluys
h. de Haven
i. de Steene Beer
k. 't Magesÿn
l. 't Rauelÿn
m. de Hooftpoort
n. 't Hooft
o. Sant berche poort
p. Willemstats poort
q. Konterscharp
r. Suÿkerberch
s. 't Hooren Werck
t. het Veer
Dyck
Dyck
Moye Keene of Roo Vaert
Pedes Geometrici
240
480

80. *Klundert, 1632* (*M. Boxhoorn*)

main lateral street at right angles. As plan *78* indicates, provision was made for all the necessary components of a garrison town: the Governor's house was placed to the west of the church and appropriate sites were allotted to the arsenal, powder magazine, hospital and even a gallows.

Willemstad is a neat little essay in Renaissance idealism in the style favoured

79. *Willemstad: harbour, dike street, main street, town hall and church*

by sixteenth-century advocates of the rectangular form of plan. It is strongly expressive of the supreme desire for symmetry in outline, in road and canal pattern and in shape of building blocks and open spaces. It displays the *sine qua non* of Renaissance idealists, the broad, central tree-lined avenue having a public building, the church in this case, set precisely on the axis as a terminating feature. It is as difficult to get into, or out of, as the ideal Renaissance fortified town for it has only one entrance by land and one by sea. Its plan was a rigid, finite conception that envisaged a static and limited population and made no allowance for future expansion. The need for expansion never arose, however, for with no sound economic basis for its foundation and in view of the proximity of established centres such as Bergen-op-Zoom and Dordrecht it could never aspire to anything beyond a local function in the field of commerce. Like many another primarily military town it was never developed to full capacity, and vacant building sites are still to be seen within its fortifications.

KLUNDERT (plan *80*) was built about the same time as Willemstad, and some ten miles east of it, in accordance with a plan that displayed the same characteristics of neatness, symmetry and completeness. A similar dike protected the town from the waterway, and a broad central canal led to two tree-lined rectangular spaces, one for town hall and market place, the other for church and churchyard. Little now remains of the original development owing to damage sustained during the last war.

COEWORDEN affords the only instance in the Netherlands of the radial-concentric form of plan so much in vogue among new-town idealists towards

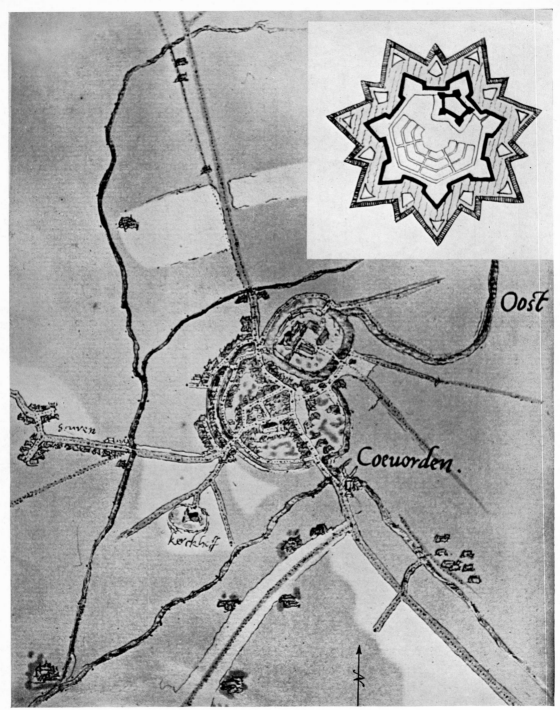

81. *Coeworden, circa 1570 (Jacob van Deventer). Inset shows layout as rebuilt 1597-1601*

the end of the sixteenth century. A settlement was in existence there as early as the eleventh century, guarding a gap in the peat moors that gave access to the Drenthe district, and it received a charter in 1395. The town as mapped by van Deventer *circa* 1550 (plan *81*) was completely destroyed by the occupying Spaniards in 1592 and was replaced in 1597–1601, with the aid of a State subsidy, by a Renaissance fortress *par excellence.* The new layout form is shown inset on plan *81* to a scale about half that of van Deventer's map. Lavedan, examining progress in theory and practice of ideal fortress planning, states that about this time the balance of opinion among defence experts favoured the radial-concentric pattern as against the rectangular, and that the realization of Scamozzi's long-discussed project for Palmanova was a cogent factor in deciding the new form for Coeworden.[3]

Perfection in defence was the principal aim of the plan; every other need was subordinated to it. About five times as much land was devoted to defence purposes as to the built-up area of the town proper. The citadel was sited on the highest ground. The adjoining market place, some three-quarters of an acre in area, was planned only incidentally as such: its more important functions were those of parade ground and assembly point for manning the bastions at a moment's notice. The streets radiating from the market place were linked by several circumferential routes, again with the object of enabling the defences to be reached by citizens in the shortest possible time. The fan-shaped street pattern still persists in the modern town, although hardly a building remains that is more than two hundred years old. The site formerly taken up by the vast defence works now makes a pleasant, if curiously shaped, open space belt but, as in the case of Naarden, Geertruidenberg, Hulst and other strongly defended places, the water defences still remain and the outlines of the great bastions and ravelins are still clearly defined.

These three new towns, although fairly typical of the Renaissance in civic design in general, were not representative of the movement in the Netherlands in particular. The strictly formal town plan beloved of the Renaissance architect apparently found little favour with Dutch city councils. Two reasons might be advanced for this. The first is that one of the least worries of the utopian architect at his drawing-board was that sufficient land would be available for his project; but in the parts of the Netherlands where money could be spared for idealistic use of space, land was only with the greatest difficulty made available for essential development. The second is that the individualist Dutch burgher would have ridiculed a notion that his house should form merely an anonymous element

123

in a monumental urban composition, least of all one designed to perpetuate the glory of a ruler. Citizens of other countries might have been content to live in reflected glory along one of the streets radiating from the palace of a despot, as at Versailles or Karlsruhe; the Dutchman preferred a more personal domestic setting. The Renaissance in town planning in the Netherlands is not therefore manifested in the building of novel forms of town, nor in set schemes of a monu-mental nature in existing towns: rather is it apparent in more refined archi-tectural style and in rational town improvements and town extensions.

ARCHITECTURE

It was not until well into the sixteenth century that the adoption of permanent materials for house building became more the rule than the exception. Pressure of demand upon buildable space within town walls made it necessary for buildings to be higher and closer together and, moreover, great fires wrought havoc among wooden and thatched constructions: major conflagrations in which more than half the built-up area was laid waste are recorded in twelve instances[4] during the fifteenth century and doubtless others went unrecorded. Town councils did all they could to encourage use of brick and tile, but had to acknowledge that the expense was beyond the means of most citizens. Wood and thatch con-struction was largely condoned, therefore, although regulations were framed with the object of reducing fire risk: no party walls were permitted, the use of tar or pitch with thatch was prohibited, and adequate firebreak spaces had to be left between adjacent buildings. Municipal firemasters appointed to enforce such rules made frequent inspections of buildings in course of construction or repair.

The two outstanding achievements of the fifteenth century, architecturally, were churches and town gates. Small, simple places of worship with which previous generations had been content now grew into, or were replaced by, spacious and lofty Gothic or traditional structures, in brick and stone, of monumental proportions as at Haarlem (55), Alkmaar, Delft, Breda and 's Hertogenbosch. Even a small town like Goes in South Beveland which had at the time probably no more than a thousand inhabitants could boast a parish church of nave dimensions some 190 feet by 90 feet and 90 feet in height; and in Alkmaar, where the population was scarcely larger, the nave of St. Laurenskerk was nearly 265 feet long. It is hardly surprising that many of these great churches are still incomplete as regards their towers. Those of Dordrecht, Wijk-by-Duurstede, Veere and Zieriksee, to name a few at random, have massive square towers that were obviously intended to carry a spire or other superstructure of considerable height, but in so many cases resources were lacking to bring the original conception to successful fruition, despite the fact that civil offences were frequently punished by fines in terms of bricks or spells of hard labour at church building. The other notable architectural achievement of the century, the massive gate set in mediaeval defence walls, was an expression of civic pride in which towns strove to outdo each other. Such examples as the Kamper-binnenpoort and Koppelpoort at Amersfoort (*65*, *68*), the Drogenapstoren (*73*) and the Berkel watergate at Zutphen, the Sassenpoort, Zwolle, the Koren-burgertoren, Nijmegen and the Amsterdamschepoort, Haarlem (*57*) are typical of the variety and versatility shown in the design of this feature. Of town halls built during the fifteenth century only a few survive, and are mostly in the Gothic tradition. Those of Veere and Gouda (*25*, *53*) show a high order of craftsman-ship, as also those of Maastricht, Tiel and Doesburg.

The sixteenth century saw the last of the pre-Reformation style in church building, as well as the last monasteries and nunneries to be built, in the northern provinces at any rate, until modern times. Pre-Reformation churches that had not been completed towards the end of the century never reached completion in the form originally envisaged, for by that time the Protestant religion had become predominant and its mode of worship called for a different functional treatment of the interior. The church at Willemstad was the first to be built in accordance with the new tradition, in which the pulpit and the organ, with pews arranged in fanwise rows around them, replaced the altar as the climax of the composition. The long cruciform shape normally associated with ecclesi-astical architecture was no longer appropriate, and gave place to square and rounded forms. Experiments were made in octagonal shapes, as with the Oost-kerk of Middelburg and the Nieuwekerk at The Hague, in circular shapes as the Ronde Luthersche kerk, Amsterdam, and with a squat cruciform shape as the Westekerk and Noordekerk, also in Amsterdam. Many former monasteries and nunneries in towns were put to other uses such as schools, barracks and hospitals; they proved particularly well suited as refuges for victims of leprosy, smallpox and other pestilences that had been the scourge of Europe since the Crusades.

The Renaissance in Dutch architecture was as gradual and unspectacular a process as was the acceptance of new ideas in town planning. The early stages witnessed remarkably little variation in the traditional size, shape and proportions of buildings other than churches. Wooden building forms were often simply repeated in stone or brick as, for example, the Scots' House at Veere (*26*) or the

82. *Amsterdam: O.Z. Voorburgwal No. 14, shop and house, circa 1600*

83. *Amsterdam: Gelderschekade 97-9, house and warehouse both circa 1600*

Gravensteen at Zieriksee. The scale and grouping of buildings, public and private alike, remained virtually as small and intimate as in mediaeval times. With the exception of Amsterdam town hall (1648-64), the building of which introduced the second phase of the architectural Renaissance, there were no secular buildings of a massively monumental nature to be found in seventeenth-century Netherlands: town halls, guild halls and the like were not much larger than houses. In fact, the only real advances brought about by the movement lay in the more widespread adoption of permanent materials, greater skill in their use, spacious and regular fenestration, and decorative additions in the form of architraves, pilasters and cornices and an interesting variety in top-gable treatment. The ideas disseminated by Hans Vredeman de Vries (1527-1604), a Dutchman living in Antwerp whose manual of designs for external decoration was extensively used by masons and carpenters, had a wide following among Dutch Renaissance architects. The leaders in the first phase, Lieven de Key (1565-1627) and Hendrik de Keyser (1565-1621), developed the typical tall, narrow, flat-fronted town house in brick, with doors framed in ornamental architraves and well-spaced casement windows surmounted by relieving arches infilled with decoration in shell and various other motifs. Only the top half of the window opening was glazed in the first instance, the remainder being protected by shutters. Cornerstones, keystones and the lines of cross-walls were picked out in natural stone, and the steep-

84. *Goes: Turfkade, Gothic house at left and others late sixteenth century; mansion at right circa 1765*

pitched roof gable was treated in stepped form, the so-called "trap-gevel", tapering to a single attic window. Thanks to solidity of construction in the first instance, and to good maintenance or skilful restoration, many such buildings survive all over the country. The Haarlem terrace (*58*) can be regarded as typical of small houses at the time, and rather larger examples are seen in photographs *38, 62, 82–4*; the stately merchant house to the right in the last-named dates from about 1765 and shows a later French influence. The same characteristics of style are also familiar in public buildings, as in the town halls of Naarden (*36*), Culemborg and Leiden, the Butchers' Hall at Haarlem and, in rather more decorative form, the St. Jans Gasthuis at Hoorn (*85*).

The building of Amsterdam's new town hall (*86*) by Jacob van Campen (1595–1657) heralded the adoption of a restrained classical style akin to palatial architecture in the Palladian tradition. Pieter Post (1608–69), Daniel Stalpaert (1615–76) and Philips Vingboons (1614–78) and his brother Justus were among the leading practitioners of the new order, in

85. *Hoorn: St. Jans Gasthuis, 1563*

which the influence of French classicism was strongly marked. The "Trippenhuis" in Amsterdam, built by Justus Vingboons about 1662, is a striking example (87). Also characteristic of the second phase of the movement was the development of various forms of gable treatment in Baroque fashion: the "trap-gevel", so popular up to about 1660,

86. *Amsterdam: Royal Palace, formerly town hall, 1648-64*

was succeeded by "klok-gevels" (88), "hals-gevels" (89, extreme left and right), "tuit-gevels" (89, second from left), "top-gevels" (89, second and third from right), and gay methods of cornice treatment (89, fourth from right). The forms illustrated are especially typical of Amsterdam, but each province, town and even village seems to have developed its own characteristic fantasies of style. Greater skill and experience in the use of glass and the adoption, about 1665, of the sash window encouraged larger window space in façades in general and, in particular, modification of earlier ground-floor elevations to give taller windows, as in photograph 83 and many other cases.

In general, business, residential and warehouse uses were all accommodated in the same building along a canalside, the ground floor being set aside for shop and office purposes, the first and second for residential and the third and attic floors for warehouse use. Along particularly valuable harbour and canal frontages, however, specially designed buildings were erected solely for warehouse

87. *Amsterdam: "Trippenhuis", circa 1662*

88. *Amsterdam: O.Z. Voorburgwal Nos. 101-7, late seventeenth-century "klokgevels"*

89. *Amsterdam: Singel Nos. 326-316, "hals", "tuit", and "top" gevels*

89a. *Detail of 89*

use; examples are those in the Brouwersgracht and the Gelderschekade, Amsterdam (*90, 83*) and similar designs are to be found in Middelburg, Zieriksee, Dordrecht, Haarlem, Leiden and elsewhere. The former warehouses of the East India Company built at Hoorn in 1606 (*91*) were very spacious and had

90. *Amsterdam: Brouwersgracht*
No. 178, warehouse circa 1630

91. *Hoorn: warehouses 1606*

a depth of some 200 feet along the return frontage of the side street. Adjacent houses along a canal were seldom the work of the same architect but, although differing in detail as regards façade and gable treatment and window and cornice lines, they usually stood as good neighbours architecturally. Building ordinances and contracts for sale of plots provided for standard plot frontages, and sometimes specified a maximum number of stories for particular localities; they also required developers to provide party walls so that terrace building could be secured, and occasionally stipulated that only certain kinds of brick or stone could be used on façade walls. Within these controls, however, architects and builders were allowed considerable latitude in elevational treatment; and that such was exercised is evident from photographs *88, 89*. One item invariably included in these tall narrow-fronted buildings, house and warehouse alike, was the pulley on the extension of the ridge pole which enabled heavy goods to be hoisted to the loft or furniture to be moved in through windows. A remarkable feature of Dutch building at this period was that the façade wall was so often not at right angles to side walls. It is particularly noticeable on corner plots, or along a street or canalside following a curved alignment, or where a "steeg" climbed up a dike berm sideways across the contours, and is illustrated in photograph *83*, which was taken square with the façades of the buildings. An exaggerated example of this curious shape of building, which gave a façade of more impressive appearance and greater window area, is the St. Jans Gasthuis at Hoorn (*85*), and it is by no means uncommon in towns elsewhere in the Netherlands.

TOWN IMPROVEMENTS

Equally unspectacular, though none the less important, were the improvements that took place in towns during the Renaissance. The "Golden Age" of prosperity saw significant changes in the urban scene. Most streets were cobbled and some widened for horsemen and coach traffic. Wooden bridges over canals were replaced by arched bridges in brick and masonry. Harbours were extended and important canals made straighter, wider and deeper. New market places were made available by filling in grachten no longer needed as circulation routes. New guild halls for various guilds, for example Butchers', Bakers', Buttermakers', Linenmakers', Clothmakers', Flaxmakers', Leathermakers', and others, were erected in prominent positions; new banks, exchanges, offices and hotels were also established in the wave of prosperity. Few major fires were recorded after the end of the century because of the prohibition of wooden and thatched buildings in central areas and of much improved organization and equipment for municipal fire brigades. A lively engraving depicting Amsterdam's new fire-fighting apparatus and an enthusiastic team of firemen in action is included in Beudeker's *Collection of Plans and Views*, 1728.[5]

REFERENCES

1. FISHER, H. A. L., *A History of Europe*, p. 463.
2. 'T HOOFT, P. J., *Dorpen in Zeeland*, 1946. Description and plan, pp. 72 *et seq.*
3. LAVEDAN, P., *op. cit.*, pp. 90–2.
4. PETERS, C. H., *op. cit.*, Vol. II, p. 461.
5. BEUDEKER, C., *Collection of Plans and Views of the United Provinces*, 1728, Vol. VII, pp. 17, 18.

CHAPTER VIII

Town Extensions

As stated in the previous chapter, a feature of particular interest in Dutch town planning of the sixteenth and seventeenth centuries was the manner in which the problem of town extension in low-lying areas was solved. It can hardly be said that these extensions were attractive in appearance for they generally contained little more than canals, streets, houses and workshops, and lacked the relief of squares, incidental open spaces and major buildings. They proved to be what they were planned to be, workmanlike additions of space for utilitarian purposes. The interest lies in the manner in which the space was gained from swampy surroundings and merged with existing development to form a single, coherent town rather than a series of unrelated appendages surrounding a mediaeval nucleus. Of several successful solutions to the problem, those of Leiden and Haarlem are discussed here and that of Amsterdam in the next chapter.

LEIDEN. The rapid growth of the city during mediaeval times has already been noted. By the end of the sixteenth century the problem of securing sufficient space to accommodate the mounting population had become acute, for no new land had been made available since 1389. Leiden's cloth industry had assumed world importance, and industrialists and merchants were constantly attracting workmen from all parts of Holland to settle in the city; the population was, moreover, increasing by migration of weavers from Flanders, France and Germany. All available space within the walls was fully developed, as plan *46* indicates, and bad slum conditions had arisen in an area half way along the Haarlemmerstraat.

The fourth extension, planned in typical grachtenstad fashion, was therefore commenced north of the encircling canal, the Oude Vest, in 1610. A long, straight canal, the Lange Gracht, was dug parallel with the Oude Vest, the latter being retained as a traffic route, and five short grachten were made to cross it and to provide links with the Oude Vest and the new encircling moat. Development on either side of the Lange Gracht was two house plots in depth and consisted almost entirely of small houses and workshops for weavers.

The fifth extension, to the east, was implemented in two phases, the first being started in 1644 and the second in 1659. The zoning plan for these areas reserved the frontages of the broad Heerengracht to high-grade commercial and residential purposes for prosperous merchants, whilst the area further east, subdivided by three canals parallel to the Heerengracht and following the routes of former polder ditches, was planned and developed with workshops and industrial housing. South of the New Rhine the New Levendaal canal, constructed in prolongation of the existing inner waterway, provided a direct link route to the central area, and satisfactory connections between the old town and the new were secured elsewhere as can be seen from plan *46*. The new streets in the industrial and high-density housing areas, indicated by dotted lines on the key of the plan, were typical of workmen's quarters in general; they formed elongated building blocks separated at intervals by narrow lanes. These extensions made seventeenth-century Leiden the largest and most important city in the Netherlands apart from Amsterdam. Its area increased from 50 acres in 1250 to 400 acres in 1660, and its population from probably less than 1,000 to 70,000 over the same period.

HAARLEM provides a remarkable instance of a late sixteenth-century "comprehensive development" scheme within the walls, followed in the next century by a considerable enlargement beyond the northern boundary.

As mentioned previously, the city had sustained much damage from bombardment during the seven-month siege of 1572–3, and the great fire of 1576 left many streets in the central and south-western areas entirely devoid of buildings. In order to ascertain the full extent of the damage the City Council caused a topographical survey to be made; and plan *54*, which was prepared from this survey in 1578, indicates how widespread the destruction was. The architect-planner Lieven de Key was instructed by the Council to prepare a redevelopment plan and, as can be seen from a map published by J. P. Saenredam in 1628,[1] the major provisions of the plan had been implemented within a span of fifty years. A more complete picture of the form which the redevelopment took is given by Pieter Wils's plan (*92*), dated 1646.

The area contained within the fifteenth-century extension had been built up, before the fire, in a somewhat casual manner, with groups of weavers' housing along winding streets interspersed with hofjes, convents, monasteries and doelen,[2] and a few undeveloped spaces remained. The redevelopment plan envisaged a more compact and economic layout comprising a series of long, narrow blocks about the axis of two long, straight canals, the Raamgracht and

133

92. *Haarlem, 1616 (Pieter Wils)*

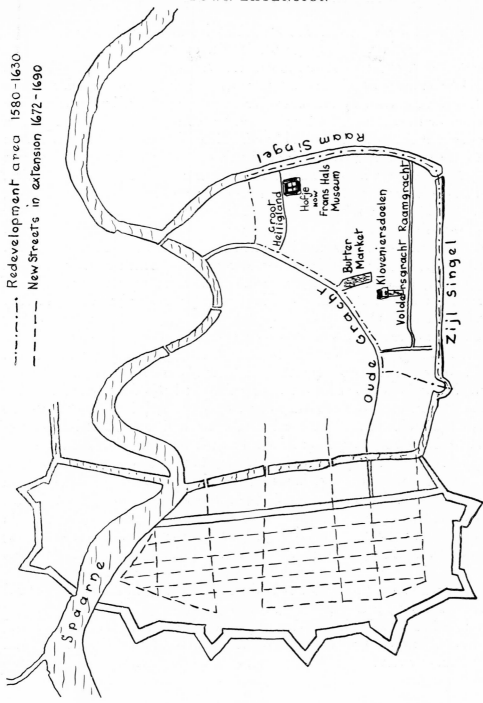

Redevelopment area 1580-1630

New Streets in extension 1672 - 1690

Raam Singel

Groot Heiligland

Hofje now Frans Hals Museum

Oude Gracht

Butter Market

Kloveniersdoelen

Voldersgracht Raamgracht

Zijl Singel

Spaarne

92a. *Haarlem. Key to 92 showing on left the later northern extension of streets and fortifications*

its continuation the Voldersgracht, as indicated on the key to plan *92*. Comparison of this plan with plan *54* shows that opportunities of straightening
out several streets and canals were not missed; and closer inspection reveals that
few of the monasteries and nunneries were allowed to retain their land: it was,
instead, incorporated with other land to serve various communal purposes including three new market places, a hospital and hofjes. The greater part of the area
as a whole was devoted to industrial housing, but other uses were not neglected:
two churches were rebuilt; a very fine hofje for old men was designed by Lieven
de Key in 1610 (it is now the Frans Hals Museum); the Kloveniers Doelen,
near the new Butter Market, was rebuilt in elegant style in 1607; and another,
the St. Joris Doelen, was retained though its grounds were later taken, during
the eighteenth century, as the site for a *proveniershuis*. All rebuilding was in
permanent materials, and the terrace in photograph *58* formed part of the scheme.
Although it cannot be said that this major redevelopment scheme resulted in
anything really outstanding in the way of development, there is little doubt of
its competency as an early example of large-scale planning and of the efficiency
with which it was put into practice.

The city's increasing industrial prosperity had attracted many settlers, and large
numbers of foreigners continued to flock there during the seventeenth century.
This was the cause of disorderly suburban "shack" development that took place
beyond the northern defence canal during the first half of the century. Some
four hundred houses, most of them in an insanitary condition, cluttered up the
area, and the problems they presented led the Council to consider inclusion of
the land within the municipal boundary. Plans for this ambitious extension had
already been drawn up by Pieter Post in 1643 but wars with England caused
them to be shelved. In 1661, however, the plan submitted by the Haarlem
architect-planner Salomon de Bray (1597–1664) received the approval of the
Council.

The "written statement" accompanying the plan contained some interesting
information as to the ways in which settlers were to be attracted to take up sites
in the new district. De Bray proposed that all persons already living within
the area, or who would undertake to build a house there, should be granted full
rights of citizenship; that, to encourage building, mortgages at low rates of interest
should be made available by the Council; that certain reliefs in taxation should
be granted in respect of goods produced in the district for sale in the city; and
that freedom of worship be accorded to all except Catholics.[3]

In January 1671 the Council made formal application to the Government of

Holland and West Friesland for permission to proceed with the plan, explaining the necessity of bringing this area, "where there is much disorder and mischief not only by night, when the gates of the city are closed, but at all times", under the control of the city and of "preventing the occupants thereof from cheating the Council of its revenue by bringing goods into the city without licence".[4] In March 1671 the approval of Government was received and the Council thereupon appointed an "Executive Authority" to implement the scheme. Notices were served upon all owners whose interests were affected and the Authority met twice weekly to hear objectors, some of whom proved obstructive. The decision was therefore taken to withhold compensation from owners of insanitary houses who had not demolished them within a specified time. By November of the same year considerable progress had been made with preliminaries: a satisfactory link between the city and the extension had been secured by means of two bridges, drainage canals were excavated and streets and plots set out, and the Council advertised its intention to sell plots by auction. Purchasers were required to enter into covenants to build houses of approved design and materials, of at least two stories, and of ground-floor height not less than twelve feet.

The scheme, which made an addition of some 450 acres to the city, was nearing completion in 1689 when Romeyn de Hooghe's large-scale map of Haarlem was published.[5] Housing is shown on this map in neat terraces with some 40 per cent of each plot left as open space. As with the Leiden extensions there was nothing imposing or decorative about the development. It can, nevertheless, be commended as a most successful example of large-scale planning efficiently implemented and capably controlled. The Council would have made a considerable profit had it not been necessary to enclose the area with extensive fortifications of "New Netherlands" type; the expense of this great undertaking placed, instead, a heavy burden of taxation upon the citizens.

Modern Haarlem has lost the characteristic appearance of a grachtenstad because so many of its former canals have been drained and built up as road-traffic thoroughfares. The Oude Gracht, which formerly defined the limits of the fifteenth-century extension, the Raamgracht and Voldersgracht, which formed the principal interior route for that extension, and the new canals dug for the seventeenth-century extension, no longer exist.

DENSITY OF DEVELOPMENT

Analysis of the Leiden extensions of 1610, 1644 and 1659, made from a large-scale map of late seventeenth-century date,[6] shows a density of development in houses per net acre of the order of 19, 13 and 23 respectively. Maps of similar date of other large and prosperous cities such as Haarlem, Gouda, Groningen and Dordrecht indicate an average standard in sixteenth- and seventeenth-century extensions of some 20 houses per net acre. Such a density resulted from the adoption of a very narrow plot frontage—15 feet was by no means unusual even for houses of the prosperous middle class—and from the invariable practice of building in long and continuous terraces. The depth of a house was generally some three times the length of its frontage, and the plot depth some six times. In the absence of detailed data relating to population it is difficult to arrive at accurate densities in terms of persons per acre. Eberstadt[7] quotes figures, for the year 1732, of persons per house in Leiden (6.42) and Haarlem (5.65) which suggest a typical density for more prosperous cities of something like 120, but this is considered to be rather on the low side.

Examination in terms of density of part of a housing project realized in Amsterdam in 1671 yields approximate figures of 19 houses or 76 habitable rooms or some 200 persons per net acre. The portion of the scheme analysed shows that 189 house plots were contained in a net area of almost exactly 10 acres. Plot frontages were generally 28.9 feet and depths averaged just over 80 feet. A description of the houses and some financial aspects of the project are contained in an article by Dr. L. van Nierop.[8] The City Council, anxious to attract weavers to Amsterdam at this time, authorized three charitable trusts to build houses for rental to anyone who would undertake this "cottage" industry. The layout plan prepared for the trustees displayed all the dull uniformity of the typical extension of a large water town. It consisted of long, narrow terraces, two house plots in depth, facing sometimes on to a canal but mostly on to streets 28 feet wide and intersected occasionally by a *steeg*. The space was entirely given over to housing with the exception of corner plots, which were allocated for use as shops, bakeries or alehouses. An important part of the preliminary site works was the sinking of 52 piles for each house. Houses were built of red brick with tiled roofs, and each comprised semi-basement, basement first floor and attic. Basement and ground floors were tiled throughout and provided separate accommodation for two families: each had an entrance hall 10 feet by 20 feet, a living-sleeping room 20 feet by $18\frac{1}{2}$ feet and a kitchen 10 feet by 18 feet.

The living-room was lit by four windows, two facing the street and two the garden, and had a fireplace and a *bedstee* (built-in beds). The kitchen was fitted with a food cupboard, a crate for peat and another bedstee. The first-floor room, extending over the living-room and entrance hall and lit by three windows at both back and front, was reached by a circular staircase from the hall. It was intended only as a workroom: the tenants installed looms there and were able to do their weaving in good conditions of light and ventilation. A ladder led from the workroom to a loft, lit by single windows back and front, where materials, cloth and finished garments could be stored. A hoist fixed outside the front window facilitated the lifting of bales of wool to workroom or store. Rainwater storage tanks were installed under the entrance stairs at back

93. *Amsterdam: Noortsche Bosch, housing, Derde Weteringdwarsst, circa 1660*

and front for each family; a privy in the garden was shared. The standard of accommodation, if humble, was at least far in advance of that which industrial workers in British towns had to tolerate two centuries later. Many of the houses are still in occupation (*93*).

In comparison with the standards advocated for the new towns of an enlightened twentieth century, the density of building adopted by seventeenth-century Dutch town planners must be regarded as high. Yet they can hardly be criticized for overbuilding. The majority of houses, whether of the prosperous middle class or of the artisan, had their own small private garden, and many faced on to a tree-lined canal. The latter, in itself, was a most valuable open space, providing a pleasant promenade in summer and a skating course in winter, and it helped to ensure the necessary light, air and space about buildings. The allocation of public open space in the form of parks and gardens on a scale now normally regarded as desirable was obviously impracticable when the cost of making land available for town extension was so great. Compact planning and a sharply demarcated "urban fence" brought the open countryside close to the town and amply compensated for the lack of amenity open space within it.

REFERENCES

1. AMPZING, S., *Beschrijving der Stad Haerlem*, 1728, contains this map, so dated.
2. See Glossary.
3. PETERS, C. H., *op. cit.*, Vol. I, p. 297.
4. PETERS, C. H., *op. cit.*, Vol. I, p. 297.
5. *Collection of Maps and Plans of the Netherlands*, British Museum (ref. Maps, 13 f 12), contains this plan, p. 30.
6. BEUDEKER, C., *op. cit.*, Vol. IV. The map is entitled *Lugdunum Batavorum*.
7. EBERSTADT, R., *Neue Studien uber Stadtebau und Wohnungswesen*, 1914, Vol. II, p. 78.
8. VAN NIEROP, L., *De Huisen in het Noortsche Bosch*, 34st. Jaarboek van het Genoot⁄ schap AMSTELODAMUM, 1937.

CHAPTER IX

Amsterdam

THE commercial capital of the Netherlands takes pride of place among her cities not only in size and importance: its early seventeenth-century development represents in conception and implementation the boldest, most extensive and most successful feat of town planning ever achieved in the country and indeed, for that period of time, in the world.

It does not rank among the older Dutch cities; Leiden, Haarlem and Delft were much larger and far more important at the date when Amsterdam first aspired to a town charter about the year 1300. During the first part of the thirteenth century it was only a small fishing village astride the banks of the Amstel near its junction with the broad river Ij, and its surroundings were bleak and boggy wastes offering little encouragement for permanent habitation. The dikes built to hold the Amstel to its course provided the only safe and firm building sites; both curved outwards on approaching the Ij, one westwards to link with the Ij dike and the other eastwards to join the Zuider Zee dike, in the manner described earlier as typical of the seaport.[1] The probable form of the village at this stage is indicated in fig. *16(a)*. In 1240 a dam constructed across the Amstel formed inner and outer harbours, the Rokin and Damrak respectively, and the main stream was divided into two channels leading to the sea as shown in fig. *16(b)*. These channels, the Oude Zijds Voorburgwal and the Nieuwe Zijds Voorburgwal, formed the boundaries of the dike-and-dam town.

The original Amstel dikes provided routes for the first long streets of the future city, the Warmoesstraat on the east and the Nieuwendijk on the west (see key to plan *98*); their origin as dike streets is demonstrated by the fact that they are much higher than surrounding streets. The narrow lanes which cross them were formerly field paths leading up from the marshy meadows, and it is noticeable that those approaching the steeper dike, the Nieuwendijk, do not meet it at right angles but at such an angle as to secure an easier ascent across the slope from the meadows. Buildings on either side of the Damrak and the Rokin originally fronted directly on to the water to permit of easier handling of goods

141

94. *Amsterdam, circa 1544 (Cornelis Anthoniszoon)*

from ships (*95*), but later, in 1526, an order was issued for the removal of canal-side privies and pigsties so that quays could be built out into the Damrak on one side and the Rokin on both sides. The dam, and an open space adjoining it, was formed into a market place that later became the civic centre and principal place of assembly (the "Dam"); the first town hall (1386) had a site on

95. *Amsterdam: Damrak, warehouses and offices, seventeenth and eighteenth centuries. Oudekerk spire in background*

its western flank. The church of St. Nicholas (1334), more commonly called the Oudekerk, was built in typical dike town tradition on lower ground behind the Warmoesstraat, and soon became surrounded by a network of narrow streets. In the fourteenth century the city began to take its share in the Baltic trade, forming commercial contacts with Stavoren and Deventer, and increased prosperity made its area of some 98 acres inadequate. Three comparatively minor extensions in 1367, 1380 and 1450 added another 350 acres within the municipal boundary. The area was closely built up in the compass of its defence palisades; most of the buildings were of wood with thatched roofs, and it is not surprising that a great fire in 1451, followed by an even greater one in the next year, left hardly a building undamaged.

With the resignation, fortitude and optimism shown by mediaeval man in face of these customary calamities, the citizens set about the task of rebuilding their premises in more durable materials, and were assisted in so doing by temporary reliefs from taxes and loans from the central government. During the years 1482–1500 the reconstructed area was for the first time enclosed by a wall with towers and gates of mediaeval design. To avoid further widespread damage by fire a building ordinance was passed in 1521 requiring the demolition of wooden and thatched houses and their replacement with brick and tile construction, but the cost of permanent materials made its provisions difficult to enforce. Another ordinance, enacted in 1533, sought to improve public health in the city. Rapid increase of population had resulted in the occupation of

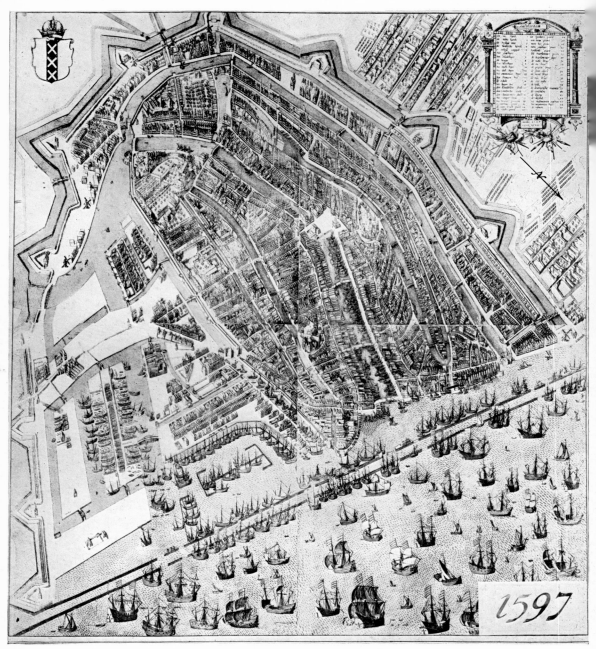

96. *Amsterdam, circa 1597 (Pieter Bast)*

single houses by two or more families and, there being no sanitary provision on upper floors, slops were disposed of by emptying buckets out of windows into the canal or street, a practice which commended itself neither to the passer-by nor to the Council. The ordinance therefore obliged houseowners to install sinks, emptied via lead soil pipes, and it also forbade the building of covered drains or sewers unless they were fitted at suitable intervals with detachable inspection covers. Privies erected alongside the city defence wall were also ordered to be removed.

The first fairly accurate idea of the appearance of the city is given by the perspective-plan made by Cornelis Anthoniszoon in 1536 of which plan 94 is a later impression. It shows the broad Singel as the western fortification canal and the Kloveniersburgwal and Geldersche Kade as the eastern limit. Inner harbours are represented as being crowded to capacity whilst many more ships appear to be awaiting their turn to enter; but whilst trade was undoubtedly expanding the amount of shipping shown is unlikely to have been so great in reality: one of the reasons for preparing such elaborate and ornamental town maps was to impress foreign merchants with the city's wealth and greatness.

On Pieter Bast's map in perspective, made half a century later (96), the Singel appears as an inner waterway and a new broad encircling canal is seen to have been dug some 150 feet further westwards. The function of this canal was primarily to drain the land and to provide clay for raising its level for building, an essential preliminary to any extension on the city's marshy environs; but it acted also as part of the defence system and details are shown of the first bastion fortifications.

Neither of these beautifully executed maps is, however, as accurate as Jacob van Deventer's preliminary sketch map (97) drawn in 1558. An interesting feature shown thereon is the pattern of the polder ditches and footpaths outside the western wall, which are seen to approach the city in parallel lines and in an approximately north-easterly direction. In later extensions this pattern was obliterated in the area between the Heerengracht and the Prinsengracht (98) and new drainage ditches and lanes were constructed at right angles to the main canals; beyond the Prinsengracht, however, the original pattern was incorporated within the urban extension, a fact which will be referred to later in this chapter.

By 1600 the city had risen rapidly to commercial supremacy not only in the Dutch Netherlands but also in Flanders. Some thirty years previously it had taken over the function of financial and commercial centre for the Low Countries from Antwerp when the latter had been almost destroyed by the Spaniards. It also received a large part of Antwerp's population as workers for its industries.

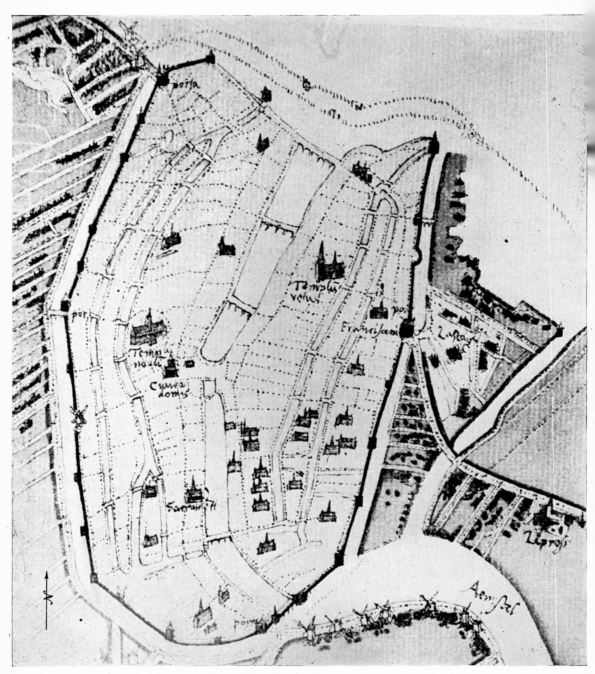

97. *Amsterdam, circa 1558 (Jacob van Deventer)*

It was now a flourishing, vigorous community of 50,000 people, ably directed by a Council composed largely of merchants who saw that at this stage their city needed a comprehensive plan to regulate and phase its future development.

The question of a major extension had already received attention from the Council during the latter half of the sixteenth century, and towards the end of that century the celebrated "plan of the three canals" was prepared by Hendrik Jz. Staets. It envisaged the digging of many miles of new canal and the preparation of 1,334 acres of land for building, thus increasing the area of the city to 1,790 acres. Although the proposals at first met with opposition from certain speculators among the Councillors who had bought up land in anticipation of development, the plan was formally approved in 1607 and permission to proceed with the first stages, together with the necessary powers for compulsory acquisition of land, was granted by the central government in 1609. Work commenced in the following year. The broad framework of the scheme is admirably illustrated on the large-scale map published by Balthasar Floriszoon van Berckenrode in 1625[2] and also on J. de Ram's map of 1681 (98). Its principal features were three very wide concentric canals, Heerengracht (dug 1585), Keisersgracht (1593) and Prinsengracht (1622), which stretched from the Brouwersgracht to the Amstel (98, key), a series of radial canals and streets forming the characteristic long and narrow building blocks, and a vast ring of fortifications of "New Netherlands" design[3] five miles in length and including twenty-six bastions and seven gates. Also reserved were sites for local churches and market places and a spacious city park, the Plantage.

The planner largely responsible for the implementation of the scheme and for much of the programming of building was the surveyor-architect Daniel Stalpaert (1615–76). His zoning plan allocated the frontages along the three monumental canals to large business houses and town houses for merchants, and the building blocks formed by the radial and circumferential canals to lower middle class and artisan dwellings. Frontages to the principal harbours and along the Brouwersgracht were reserved mostly for warehouses. An extensive area to the west, the Jordaan, was zoned for industry and certain charitable bodies were to be granted sites there. It was unfortunate that the Council did not acquire this area: it was instead purchased by a group of merchants as a speculation and developed with narrow canals and streets which followed the pattern of the original polder ditches and footpaths. It lies at a noticeably lower level than adjacent areas because the developers did not trouble to prepare the land, in the manner customary in the City, by building it up with sand to a surface level of

98. *Amsterdam, 1681 (J. de Ram)*

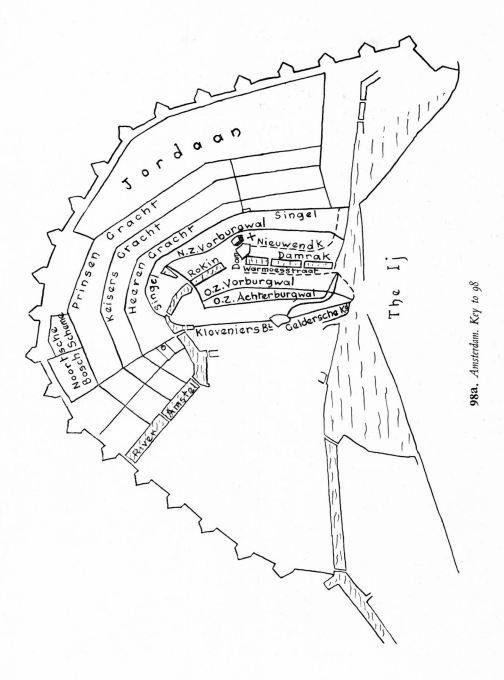

98a. *Amsterdam. Key to 98*

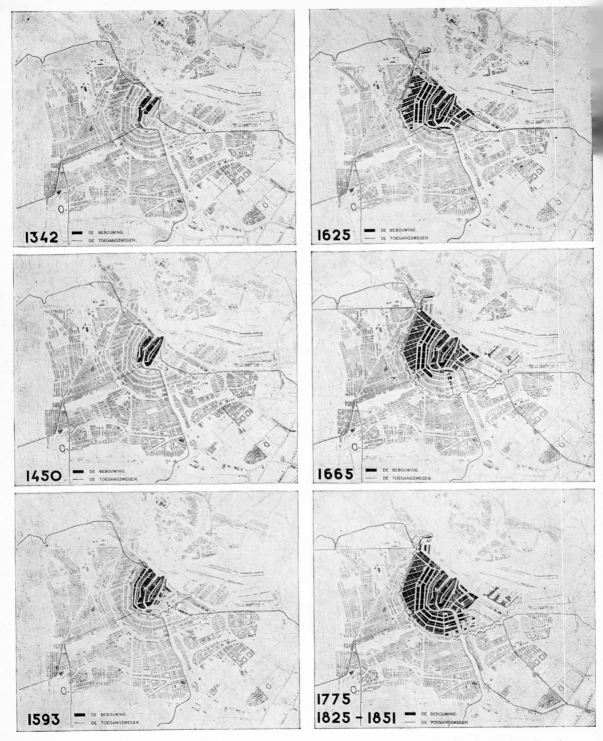

99. *Amsterdam: growth of built-up area shown superimposed on a plan of the modern city (1950). The dark lines show the principal road approaches (Department of Public Works, Amsterdam)*

70 cm. above Amsterdam datum. Cheap and crowded houses were provided there for the many immigrant workmen, particularly French Protestants and Spanish and Portuguese Jews, who could find no better accommodation. It started as, and has continued to be, the city's slum area. It should be said, however, that the dreariness of nineteenth-century big-city slums is not so marked in the district; there is a liveliness of colour and a wide variety in gable treatment; and many hofjes—a particularly delightful one built in restrained classical style by Daniel Stalpaert in 1650—afford some relief in the otherwise dull street pattern.

With the exception of the Jordaan, Stalpaert's zoning plan was successfully implemented because the Council exercised its powers of compulsory purchase of land as it became necessary for the various phases of the scheme. Having acquired an area, they prepared the land for building, divided it into plots of suitable size and shape and sold these in the open market subject to special conditions. Purchasers had to enter into covenants, which bound their successors in title also, to the effect that the land would not be put to other than stipulated uses, that plot coverage would be kept within prescribed limits, that the plot would not be subdivided by lanes or alleyways, that party wall connections would be afforded to developers of adjacent plots, and that only certain types of brick would be used for external walls.[4] New development was further regulated by the Building Ordinance of 1565 which, incidentally, proved so valuable and comprehensive an instrument that it remained in force until the early nineteenth century. It required, inter alia, that piling foundations had to be approved by municipal inspectors before building could commence; that each plot should have its own privy; and that streets and footpaths made up by the Council had to be paid for by plotholders, the cost being related to the length of frontage. A later ordinance enabled the Council to recover the costs, again on a frontage basis, of providing stone retaining walls along the canal sides.

Control of development was strictest in the areas between the three great concentric canals. Here the plot sizes averaged 26 feet frontage and 180 feet depth, and the prescription of a minimum distance of 160 feet between the backs of buildings resulted in a minimum garden length of 80 feet for each plot. A maximum site coverage of 56 per cent was thus secured. A typical set of conditions of sale, published in 1663,[5] stipulated that the following trades could not be carried on within the area: blacksmith, brewer, cooper, dyemaker, glassblower, gluemaker, soapboiler, stonecutter, sugar manufacturer and similar noxious or noisy occupations. It is remarkable that these restrictions have remained in force there ever since. The "Building Order" for the same district required, *inter alia*, that outside walls be constructed only in Lekse, Leytse, Vechtse or Rijnse bricks, and that only blue or Bremen stone could be used for drains.

So rarely are buildings of less than three stories to be seen in this area that the existence of some form of municipal control to secure a minimum, as well as a maximum, height might be presumed. Investigation has so far yielded no evidence of such control, and it is unfortunate that most of the city's older records perished in three major fires; but land values along such important frontages doubtless induced developers to obtain the maximum return in lettable space.

The implementation of the Amsterdam extension plan, and to a lesser extent those of Haarlem, Leiden and other prospering cities, has two aspects that call for special mention. One is the rapidity with which the plan was translated into reality; the other is the high degree of homogeneity and architectural good manners that characterized the resulting development. Rapidity was accounted for by the wave of prosperity that flowed into the city during the "Golden Age"; it created a steady demand for accommodation from the affluent middle classes as also from artisans and labourers attracted in ever-increasing numbers by the magnet of industrial prosperity. Homogeneity in building style and architectural good manners expressed to so great an extent were even more remarkable when it is considered that practically no building work was undertaken by the local authority which, as such, did not enter the field of housing until two centuries later. The greater part of the work was accomplished by private enterprise, generally by individuals building for themselves, sometimes by individuals or small groups as an investment for letting, occasionally by charitable bodies in the building of hofjes, or by large industrial or commercial concerns wishing to provide housing for employees and, comparatively rarely, by housing societies in schemes such as the Noortsche Bosch. It says much for the wisdom and efficiency of planning control, as exercised in covenants and leases and by a vigilant local authority, that such an extensive area of land was developed in a manner which enabled each building to retain an individuality of character and yet secured so pronounced a unity and cohesion over the area as a whole.

A measure of the success that attended this great development plan is afforded by the figures of increase in the city's population:[6] from 50,000 in 1600 it rose to 170,000 in 1650 and 200,000 in 1700. That such heavy demands for accommodation of all kinds could be satisfied in so short a period is impressive enough for the first half of the seventeenth century; but when it is realized that before a brick could be laid the land had to be drained, raised and consolidated, and that many thousands of piles had to be driven through great depths—as much as 60 feet in places—down to the level of the sand, the achievement is still more to be wondered at. Fig. *99* indicates the various stages of development that took place from the fourteenth to the seventeenth centuries superimposed on the present-day map, and gives a good impression of the way in which the plan formulated nearly three and a half centuries ago influenced the development of the modern city.[7] Nor was its realization the fruit of autocratic rule as was the Brussels of Napoleon or the Paris of Haussmann; it was the product of far-sighted citizen government in a city that has always been noted for its freedom —in trade, in religious toleration and in opening its gates to immigrants. It is the classic example of bold, competent and effectively administered town planning.

REFERENCES

1. *Supra*, p. 46.
2. See D'Ailly's catalogue, No. 112.
3. *Supra*, p. 116.
4. EBERSTADT, R., *op. cit.*, p. 38.
5. EBERSTADT, R., *op. cit.*, p. 414.
6. Figures supplied by the Gemeentarchivaris, Amsterdam, 1954.
7. Map contained in *Amsterdam*, published by Dept. of Public Works, Amsterdam, for the XXth International Congress for Housing and Town Planning, 1950.

CHAPTER X

Comparisons and Conclusions

ALTHOUGH so abstract a conception as national character cannot be adequately or accurately considered in a few words, it can at least be said of the Dutch people throughout history that they showed themselves to be hardy, hardworking, independent and individualist. Their courage and endurance in the face of the onslaughts of their greatest enemy, the sea, brought about an astonishing change in the geography of the low-lying regions of their land. As the old saying expresses it, "God created the rest of the world but the Dutch made Holland".

With unflagging energy and patience they applied themselves to the heavy tasks of pushing back the sea and draining lakes and marshes to form highly productive pasture and arable lands. They disciplined mighty and unpredictable rivers into major commercial highways by diking and damming and driving them into convenient courses and diverting their surplus waters into a complex system of internal trade routes. They constructed harbours to further their role as carriers for Europe's merchandise. Such great tasks demanded communal effort, which led to increasing freedom from feudal ties and produced a people imbued with a sense of personal liberty and capable of looking after themselves. The power of government, though vesting nominally in ducal rulers, passed early into the hands of merchant citizens serving on town councils. The people developed an extraordinary adaptability and resilience in recovering from the catastrophes and setbacks which the forces of nature periodically thrust upon them. Dordrecht's citizens, for instance, had to adjust themselves to some remarkable topographical changes. Originally traders in a river port, they reorganized their city as a market and terminating point for overland traffic when the damming of the Meuse in the fourteenth century brought an extensive area of agricultural land within the orbit of their influence. The great flood of 1421 tore away this polderland, leaving the city isolated, severed from land traffic and accessible only by water. Yet within a generation or so it had regained its former prosperity and soon rose to even greater heights in the world of commerce.

It is, perhaps, to be expected of a people constantly preoccupied with the struggle for physical and economic existence that they did not develop a high sense of the artistic in town building. The picturesque, informal, apparently undesigned beauty so often characteristic of mediaeval towns in other countries of Europe is, in general, only to be found in those Dutch towns which were sited upon naturally high ground. Equally rare is the exercise in civic design which had as its objective the attainment of a particular architectural effect and which placed aesthetic considerations above all others. The appearance of Dutch towns up to the end of the seventeenth century was not beautiful in the sense of possessing grace and elegance or of giving intellectual delight, but rather in the sense of fitness to the end in view. To make an analogy in terms of landscape, their beauty lay not in the formal symmetry of the Versailles of Le Nôtre nor in the studied irregularity of the Blenheim of "Capability" Brown, but in the simple, orderly attractiveness of a well-tended agricultural countryside.

In its general characteristics the Dutch town of mediaeval origin was orderly, functional and compact. The first of these attributes is amply illustrated by the plans contained in the present work: most of the towns portrayed bear witness to careful setting out, both on the plan and on the ground. Nor is neatness of the plan merely the neatness of a cartographer concerned with presenting his subject in the most attractive light. A recent aerial photograph of Sloten (*12*) bears an astonishing resemblance to the layout as portrayed in the map of 1622 (*10*); and although many of the buildings have been reconstructed on the same pile foundations during the three hundred years that separate these representations, it is abundantly clear that the basic plan has remained unchanged; the back land to the east of *Dubbel Straet* has been developed with a row of houses and a few more buildings added here and there, but the layout of today is substantially that of three or even six centuries ago. The same is true of many other towns; a flight over the Netherlands in a slow aircraft reveals how surprisingly little the urban pattern of the seventeenth century has altered.

The second attribute emerges from a study of the use zoning pattern of the Dutch town up to the end of the seventeenth century. It is true that a clear demarcation between industrial and residential use did not exist, but it hardly existed in any town anywhere until the twentieth century. It was common practice for the artisan to have his workshop on his house plot; "cottage industry" was the basic order of breadwinning in Britain up till the nineteenth century as it was in seventeenth-century Amsterdam;[1] collective labour in "Dark Satanic Mills" was a product of the Industrial Revolution.

155

The principal source of industrial power was the turret windmill, having the machinery housed in a fixed tower and the sails and connecting gearing in a revolving turret at the top. Windmill power facilitated the grinding of grain, spices and gunpowder, the crushing of iron ore, sawing of timber, pulping of rags for paper milling, beating of hides in tanneries and many other industrial processes. The industrial windmill was not normally sited within a town, and Dutch cities were thus relieved of much of the unpleasantness of concentrated large-scale industrial activity within their confines although they hummed with the activity of small-scale undertakers such as spinners, weavers, clothmakers, fullers, dyers, furniture makers, silversmiths, goldsmiths and the like.

Zoning for commercial use is clearly apparent. Valuable sites such as those along main navigable canals, along harbour dikes, near the bridge carrying the main road over the principal waterway, or flanking the market place were taken up by the chief public and private business uses, the weighing hall, market halls, guild halls, merchants' offices, warehouses and shops. Residential areas, together with associated uses like local churches, monasteries, convents, hospitals, hofjes and doelen, were grouped away from the areas in which the town made the greater part of its living, that is, away from the harbour quay or the principal trade lifeline or the market place. The various zones were closely knit together by road and canal communications which made the town centre always readily accessible. Extensions made from time to time were separated from each other by broad drainage canals with only occasional bridge crossings, so that conditions were created for local community life in "neighbourhood units", although such units may not have possessed all the physical components or the balance of income groups which are considered desirable in modern planning practice. But the northern extensions of Leiden, for example, contained well-defined communities of weavers each with its own church and local shops, and the same is true of the Haarlem extensions.

The third attribute of compactness does not imply a tendency to overbuilding and a shortage of open space. Study of sixteenth- and seventeenth-century town plans shows a density seldom in excess of five houses to the net acre in small towns and rising to twenty in large cities; and although most towns were enclosed during the seventeenth century with wall and moat fortifications that constituted a definite and incontestable obstacle to expansion it is remarkable how few found it necessary to extend beyond these limits until modern times. The impression of compactness was given by the long and continuous terraces of buildings. True to mediaeval tradition the terrace was the normally accepted form of development, and an observer in the street would see practically no space spared for ornamental or amenity purposes. But behind most houses was a long narrow garden where the townsman, still a countryman at heart, could grow his few flowers, herbs or vegetables or sit in the shade of his orchard trees; and an inconspicuous archway along the street frontage would often give access to a quiet little precinct of houses surrounding a green, as the Bagijnhof at Amsterdam or the hofjes all over the Netherlands. Dutch town houses have been well described as "unpretentious examples of honest building". In familiar red brick and tile, tall, narrow, flat-fronted, with steep gables and spacious windows, they were nothing if not solid and enduring, as the paintings of Pieter de Hoogh and Jan Vermeer express to perfection. Because local timber had always been scarce, permanent materials had been taken into use in the Netherlands somewhat earlier than, for example, in Britain; while half-timbered construction was still popular in Elizabethan England the Dutch had evolved a domestic style in sound, simple terraces of the kind illustrated in photograph 58. This accounts for the fact that so many of their buildings still remain in sixteenth-century dress.

Although a religious people, the Dutch never attained in their Gothic church building the artistry so eloquently achieved by the French or the Flamands. An eminent Victorian architect, though conceding their proportions to be good, went so far as to describe the great churches of Delft and Haarlem as "vast warehouses of devotion and utter failures as works of art".[2] If indeed severe, unadorned and somewhat utilitarian—the brick of which they were mostly built did not permit of much decoration or tracery—they were noble in dimensions, commanding in mass and magnificent in silhouette, and their sober lines provide yet another reflection of the character of the people for whom they were built. They were not, in general, accorded the position of prominence that the principal church in mediaeval European towns normally enjoyed, but were placed below the main dike street or away from the market place. Such siting is apparent in Amsterdam, Leiden and Enkhuisen. Those which had a central position gained it rather by accident than design: St. Bavo at Haarlem, St. Joris at Amersfoort and St. Michael at Zwolle were already established when the towns were quite small. In a number of cases, notably at Gouda and Culemborg, the church was deliberately separated from the market place by building a row of shops in front of it. This action may have been taken with the spiritual motive of preserving the dignity of the building by isolating it from the bustle of everyday life, or with the more mundane motive of creating a valuable shopping frontage.

The town hall almost invariably qualified for an important central site and, as seen from some of the illustrations in this book, was of attractive architectural style. But the building was seldom of massive proportions, and its function was not emphasized by setting it in an imposing square. It was often just another building along a dike street or canal-side, giving the impression of serving the community rather than dominating it.

Pretentious monuments had no place in Dutch cities. Ornamental fountains, obelisks, impressive equestrian statuary or triumphal arches were, and still are, quite alien to the people. The few statues of eminent citizens to be seen out of doors seem to stand with some discomfiture in not very appropriate positions. Sculptural monuments to great Dutchmen, particularly stadhouders and admirals, are mostly to be found in the principal churches of the larger cities. The pious monuments so beloved of mediaeval Christians, the market cross and the statue of the Virgin, are seldom seen north of the Meuse although they survive in towns of the southern provinces, such as 's Hertogenbosch and Bergen-op-Zoom, which remained largely Catholic. The only monuments to temporal greatness were town gates, and these were often of mighty proportions as in Zieriksee, Kampen, Zwolle, Sneek and Haarlem; but they were symbolic of the strength of the community as a whole and not of its individual citizens. They afforded powerful terminating vistas to main streets, as at Zutphen, Hoorn and Enk-huisen.

Larger cities of the Netherlands display none of the examples of luxurious architectural taste as practised in sixteenth-century Italy and imported into France and Britain during the two centuries following by noblemen and gentle-men inspired by the "Grand Tour". They possess no symmetrical, formal squares flanked by buildings of uniform façade, no grand vistas, no great palaces or processional highways designed to impress the majesty of a ruler upon a meekly acquiescent people; they give no example of the architectural set-piece composition. Even if the necessary space had been available for such ambitious schemes they would have been out of place in sturdily independent merchant communities. Two other reasons may be adduced for their absence: monumental planning was normally carried out by an autocratic government or by a powerful nobility which the Netherlands never really had; and the country was engaged in a long and hard war with Spain whilst these ideas of town planning were crystallizing in Northern Europe.

It is of interest to examine some of the results of the work of Dutch town builders by means of comparison with those of their contemporaries in Britain and elsewhere, although direct comparison is only really appropriate in the case of Dutch towns built upon sites above normal flood level: the grachtenstad, as a peculiarly Dutch conception, must be put in a class by itself.

The mediaeval "garden city", which has been described by Abercrombie,[3] Mears,[4] and others, certainly has its counterparts in the Netherlands. Houses situated in long, narrow plots are as familiar a feature of the early dike town or the bastide as of the twelfth-century British "burgh"; the large garden plot played an indispensable part in the life of the inhabitants, whose activities in the main were as tillers of the soil rather than urban wage-earners. Speed's plan of Carnarvon[5] shows a layout for this bastide similar in scale and character to those of the Netherlands in general and to the plan of Bredevoort[6] in particular. The only differences are that the building blocks in Carnarvon were built up on three sides only whilst those of Bredevoort were developed on all four, giving a desirable continuity of façade; and that, as indicated on Speed's map, casual ribbon development had begun to take place along the main roads outside the walls even before the land inside was fully utilized, whereas at Bredevoort the broad defence moat confined building within the planned limits and gave an admirably defined line of demarcation between town and countryside. The nieuwesteden extensions of Culemborg and Zutphen, with their open development of large square building blocks and abundance of gardens and orchards, were prominent among other Dutch towns which qualified for the description "garden city".

Deventer and Salisbury have some points in common though they differ fundamentally in origin and function. The former was a river port situated at a point where sea and river traffic met. The latter was planned as a new town in 1220 and became the administrative centre for a wide agricultural area. Both were cathedral cities, with the cathedral in each case standing in its own close slightly apart from the rest of the town; and both were market and commercial centres also, and had large market places. Their seventeenth-century plans show general resemblance in the rectangular street pattern and long, narrow building blocks; but it is a curious reversal of national characteristics that, whilst the diverted waters of the Avon flowed in small canals down every street in Salisbury, the Dutch town did not possess a single internal waterway. Speed's plan of Salisbury[7] shows the encroachment of several buildings on the market place, but the encroachments were only temporary and are not seen on later maps. Deventer's market place, dominated by the fine weighing hall, is still as open and spacious today as the plan (74) shows it to be. The density of building in each town at the time when the plans were drawn appears to be of much the same order, namely about five houses per net acre.

The ports of Veere and Hull show quite a pronounced resemblance in layout, as seen from a comparison of plan *23* and Wenceslaus Hollar's plan of *circa* 1665. Hull was planned at the order of Edward I in 1293—when it was renamed Kingston-upon-Hull—along the south bank of the river Hull at the place where it entered the broad waters of the Humber, and a channel dug from the western extremity of the quay south-eastwards and thence north-eastwards to the Humber afforded water protection on all sides in a similar manner to that shown for Veere on plan *23*. In both cases the long, broad quay was devoted to commercial uses and developed at a fairly high density. Both plans also show a system of streets, mostly about 18 feet in width, connecting the quay with the less densely built-up "garden city" residential area. Edward's great church of the Holy Trinity was sited well back from the commercial area, as was also the case with the Ons Lieve Vrouwe Kerk in Veere, and each town was provided with adequate market facilities. It is of interest that the gates in both cases were placed in similar positions; but it is also a testimony of the times in each country that whereas in 1665 Hull still retained its out-of-date mediaeval walls and high watch towers, Veere had been obliged at least thirty years previously to invest in expensive bastion fortifications of "Old Netherlands" type.

It is not claimed that the water town is an exclusively Dutch conception. On the contrary, the practice of founding settlements amid water or marshland, either to seek protection or to gain trading advantages, goes back into pre-history, as witness the lake settlements of Glastonbury or Geneva. The most celebrated water settlement, Venice, is at least two centuries older than any Dutch water town, and Bruges was in its prime long before Leiden or Delft had passed out of the village stage. It can be said, however, that nowhere else in the world of the Middle Ages was the reclamation of land for town building carried out on such a large scale and with such success as in the Netherlands. The grach-tenstad plan, devised and developed by Dutchmen as the only practicable means of town building in the unaccommodating terrain of their low-lying provinces, was adapted for use in other countries where similar problems of site development obtained. Dutch town planners had gained a deservedly high reputation not only for skill in control of water and in introducing it into the urban composition both as a feature of beauty and a means of transportation: they were also acknow-ledged masters of the art and practice of town fortification, having acquired their skill in the field of bitter experience against the Spaniards. Their services were, in consequence, much sought after in seventeenth-century Europe, particularly in Scandinavia, Germany and Poland, and their influence extended as far afield as St. Petersburg.

Christian IV of Denmark (1588–1648), a vigorous improver of old towns and prolific builder of new ones, relied almost exclusively upon the advice of Dutch architects and engineers for the preparation of urban development plans throughout his territories which, at that time, embraced parts of Norway, Sweden and Schleswig. Major projects for his capital, Copenhagen, were largely drawn up by Dutchmen. Hans Steenwinckel the Elder designed the arsenal (1590) on Slotsholmen Island, the new market place and its surroundings (1606) and the residential district of Nyboder (1614). Jan Semp was responsible for the "new town", now suburb, of Christianshavn (1636), an extensive area lying south-eastwards across the water from the old city, drained by canals and surrounded with a ring of bastion fortifications. Steenwinckel the Younger designed the fine Bourse, a typical product of the Dutch architectural Renaissance in a most appropriate canal-side setting. Hendrik Ruse added the "new town" of Frederikshavn (*circa* 1660) northwards of the arsenal. Among other towns which owe their plans to Dutchmen were Christianopel, Christianstad, Bredsted and Christiansand.[8] Fredericia, the fortress port of Jutland, laid out shortly after the death of Christian IV, with broad internal waterways and "Old Netherlands" fortifications was very reminiscent of the grachtenstad; so also was the great Swedish port of Gothenburg, planned at the order of Gustavus Adolphus in 1619, with its many canals, long narrow building blocks and continuous waterfront façades.

In discussing grachtensteden outside the Netherlands mention should be made of one of the most striking examples of all, which was taking shape from 1619 onwards at a distance of some ten thousand miles from the homeland. Batavia (now Jakarta), the great Dutch colonial capital, was planned to the south of a citadel sited to control the entry of a broad river into the sea. The first part of the town, covering an area of some seventy acres on the east bank of the river, was laid out as a typical water town with a rectangular network of canals and streets enclosing long, narrow building blocks. As in Amsterdam and elsewhere, the level of the land had to be raised with soil excavated from canals before building could take place. The principal street, the Prinsestraat, had the citadel as its northern terminating vista, and its southern end opened into the spacious civic and market square with the town hall as the terminating feature. Later extensions were made to the south and on the west bank of the river which more than trebled the city's area and were planned on similar lines. The river separating the two parts was neatly channelled and its banks planted with decorative shade trees, and the whole area was encircled by fortifications and singels. A detailed description of the stages of development is given by H. A. Breuning in *Het Voormalige Batavia*.

If a study of Dutch town planning is rewarding for its academic interest alone, some aspects of its achievements are not without relevance to planning practice today despite the fact that, as far as the present study goes, these achievements are three or four centuries old.

In the more densely populated parts of sixteenth-century Netherlands about 30 per cent of the people lived in towns, an exceptionally high proportion for that period in any country.[9] Dependence upon the outside world, forced on the Dutch by their country's poverty in natural resources, had produced a large merchant and industrialist class, and hence a large urban population. The aristocracy, also, were predominantly urban; they did not possess vast rural estates as did their contemporaries elsewhere in Europe. The gap between ruler and ruled, between aristocrat and common citizen, was not nearly so pro-nounced in the Netherlands as, for instance, in France or Germany; the rich of Holland were never so arrogant, the poor never so abject. From the sociological point of view, the success of a town plan can be judged by the extent to which it produces an environment conducive to family and community life. One look at an old Dutch city or town will suffice to show that the dominating com-ponent in its structure was the house, the solid, undemonstrative, homely house, built to last, like the family, for many generations. The ruler's palace, if it merited such a name, did not stand in majestic aloofness, but side by side with houses of the burghers along the same placid waterfront or in the same street or square. William the Silent's residence, the Prinsenhof, at Delft, was a case in point. Artisans' houses, if not jostling with those of more wealthy citizens, were not cut off in shabby isolation. Houses of the common man were never swept away to make space for a processional highway or a monumental piazza. The large number of charitable foundations like hofjes, proveniershuisen and weeshuisen (orphanages), whose attractive style and solid construction were so far removed from the grim degradation of the workhouse, attest to the fact that human values were held in high esteem. The whole appearance of the town, and its small, compact and intimate scale, reflected an innate respect for the dignity of the family and the community. Its internal waterways constituted coherent, but not restraining, boundaries to "neighbourhoods"; all neighbourhoods were held together in a bond of common citizenship by the defence moat.

If Dutch town builders up to the seventeenth century were not brilliantly distinguished in the field of architectural achievement, they were second to none in the technics of urban development. Their resourcefulness in the control of water and expert adaptation to building purposes of dreary and difficult sites need no further emphasis. It is remarkable that great increases in the area of the country itself, as well as of its population, produced so few new towns after the Middle Ages. The fact is attributable in part to technical skill in town exten-sion. No matter how discouraging the surrounding terrain might be for habita-tion, if a town were faced with the alternatives of extension or yielding to a rival, it extended. And enlargement did not amount merely to addition of houses and workshops in shapeless slabs of suburbia; new areas were tightly integrated with the existing nucleus by skilful re-routeing of major drainage canals, the provision of additional grachten and the building of necessary bridges, so that they became integral parts of the town itself, branches of the same tree. In the simple essentials of civic design, architectural treatment of contrasting spaces created by canal and street, use of precinct forms for privacy and repose, urbane continuity of terrace development, introduction of varying ornamental styles for individual buildings without loss of continuity in the terrace as a whole, the grace of shade trees reflected in still waters, the decided separation between town and countryside, there is ample precept for the modern planner.

Finally, it may occasion some surprise that the Dutch people, whose character bears such strong traits of individualism and conservatism, should have accepted the principle of control of development in the interests of the community and in accordance with a comprehensive town plan. The explanation may be that a people whose ancestors built the dikes and struggled to hold them against an age-long enemy inherited the tradition of acting in concert for the common good; or that the task of draining land and preparing it for building was beyond the capacity of individuals; or that the prudent Dutchman, accustomed to looking to, and planning for, the future, saw in the orderly development of his town a sound and secure field for investment. Whatever the cause, it remains a fact that town planning was a recognized and active part of Dutch local government well over three centuries ago. Just how active is demonstrated by the conception and implementation of the Amsterdam plan, or the less spectacular though equally effective Haarlem, Leiden or Groningen plans. In each case, the consultants' scheme had to pass the critical examination of the local authority and the equally interested central government. It had to be phased, and geared to the speed at which public works, the preparation of land, canals and roads, could be accom, plished. It had to be enforced by means of covenants, conditions of sale, building orders and bye-laws. It had to be implemented partly by loan from the central government but mostly with the capital of the businessman. That plans for so distant a future were brought to fruition is evidence of their basic soundness, of their general acceptance by the majority of citizens and of the confidence they inspired in investors. The art of town planning has been defined as the art of creating the kind of environment needed to produce and maintain human values, which means, *inter alia*, the balancing and harmonizing of public and private needs so that one shall not be sacrified to the other.[10] If any urban activity can be said to have approached that ideal, it was the making of Dutch towns.

REFERENCES

1. Cf. Noortsche Bosch scheme, *supra*, p. 138.
2. FERGUSSON, J., *History of Ancient and Mediaeval Architecture*, 1893, Vol. II, p. 206.
3. ABERCROMBIE, P., *Town and Country Planning*, 1943, p. 47.
4. MEARS, F., *The Planning of Mediaeval Cities*, Town Planning Institute Journal, Vol. X, No. 1.
5. SPEED, J., *Theatre of Great Britain*, 1676.
6. See British Museum reference: Maps 13 f 12.
7. SPEED, J., *op. cit.*
8. LAVEDAN, P., *op. cit.*, describes these, pp. 249 *et seq.*
9. FOCKEMA ANDREAE, S. J., *op. cit.*, p. 124.
10. ADAMS, T., *Outline of Town and City Planning*, 1936, p. 134.

APPENDIX

Sixteenth- and Seventeenth-century Cartography in the Netherlands

As old maps and plans afford such a valuable source of information in the study of the history of town planning, brief reference is made here to some of the more important of those published in the Netherlands during the sixteenth and seventeenth centuries.[1]

JACOB VAN DEVENTER (*c.* 1510–75). Van Deventer ranks first among the sixteenth-century cartographers of the Netherlands. His contemporaries considered him to be "a very great geographer", and this reputation has not dwindled. There are grounds for assuming that he studied under the famous mathematician Gemma Frisius, for he employed the same survey methods of fixing station points by triangulation as were proposed in the treatise *Libellus de locorum describendorum ratione*, published by Frisius in 1533. In that work is described the method by which the location of prominent church towers in Louvain, Malines and other towns could be determined, without the necessity of visiting them, by observing bearings to each of them from towers in Brussels and Antwerp, the bearing and distance between these two points of observation being known.

During the years 1557–75, van Deventer surveyed and mapped five provinces of the Netherlands but his most interesting achievement, as far as town planners are concerned, was the series of plans of more than two hundred towns in the Low Countries which he prepared at the commission of Philip II of Spain. The originals are held in the National Library at Madrid, but the Royal Library at Brussels has a duplicate, almost complete, set. A series of prints of North Netherlands towns was made by the Dutch printer M. Nijhoff in 1916–23, sets of which are available in the Technical High School Library, Delft, the Royal Library, The Hague, and in the British Museum Maps Library. The dots shown on these prints along the centre of each street (see plan *71*) were made from pin-pricks through the original survey plotting, and served as guide lines from which fair copies were drawn in the sixteenth century.

Van Deventer was consistent as regards presentation. Though his plans were not intended to be works of art, they were workmanlike. They were drawn freehand, in ink, tinted in water colours and always orientated so that north coincided with the top of the sheet; the scale was seldom much more or less than 1/8,000. His attention to detail was not always thorough, which is hardly surprising in view of the great distances he had to travel and the vast amount of work he produced. In small or unimportant towns the detail is rather sketchy, as in the case of Grootebroek (7) where it is rather difficult to tell whether the scribbles represent houses or trees (they are, in fact, intended to show houses). Streets and lanes are shown as being of equal width when this is not always so, and street building lines and interior detail of building blocks are often incorrectly indicated. Nevertheless there is no doubt as to the great historical value of this unique series of plans, affording as it does so remarkable a record of the layout of Dutch towns at so comparatively early a period in history.

BRAUN AND HOGENBERG. The town atlas *Civitates Orbis Terrarum*[2] edited by G. Braun (1541–1622) and engraved mostly by F. Hogenberg (1542–1600) is not confined only to the Netherlands but includes selected towns in Britain, France, Belgium, Germany, Italy, Spain and even further afield. It was published in six volumes between 1572 and 1618. Popham, in a short article,[3] considers that the majority of the bird's-eye views of Dutch and Flemish towns are no more than copies of the manuscript atlas of Jacob van Deventer, a fact of which Braun made no acknowledgment. A characteristic of plans in this series are the figures of a man and a woman which appear at the edge (see plans *49* and *64*); these were included to illustrate local costumes and also to prevent the Turk, whose religion prohibited pictorial representation of the human figure, from using the plans against Christendom. The standard of workmanship is high and detail is shown with considerably more accuracy than in van Deventer's work. The scale, however, varies from one map to another, and orientation is not always such that the direction north-south coincides with the sides of the sheet.

PIETER BAST (*d.* 1605). The few town maps that Bast produced towards the end of the sixteenth century were masterpieces of the art of engraving, demonstrating accuracy, clarity and delightful decoration. His known works, all bearing dates between 1594 and 1602, are Middelburg, Dordrecht, Amsterdam, Franeker, The Hague, Emden, Leiden and Leeuwarden. He made also several engravings of town scenes, notably a vivid prospect of the Amsterdam waterfront from the Ij. Not being a surveyor, he used existing maps as a basis for his own, but was not content merely to copy and embellish. He visited the towns to verify detail, and made amendments and additions occasioned by new development His plans thus have a special value as historical records.

BALTHASAR FLORISZOON VAN BERCKENRODE (1591–1644). Two known and important works of this brilliant engraver, completed *circa* 1625, were the large and accurate maps of Amsterdam and Rotterdam. The scale of each was about 1/1,920. In 1620, the young Leiden professor Marcus Boxhoorn published a town atlas *Theatrum Hollandiae Comitatus et Urbium nova Descriptio* which contained five topographical maps and some forty town and village plans. No indication of the identity of the author is given on any of the plans, but it is considered that most can be attributed to van Berckenrode. An edition of these plans dated 1632 is available in the British Museum Library.

JOANNES BLAEU (1596–1673). His very important work *Stedenatlas van de Vereenigde Nederlanden* was to form part of a world atlas which, however, never reached completion. The two volumes devoted to the Netherlands, the land of his birth, were published first about 1648. They contain not only topographical maps and town plans but also drawings of prominent buildings in towns, fortification systems and urban scenes. The town plans of the Netherlands are grouped in order of size and importance within the provinces in which they are situated.[4] Blaeu admitted that to publish a record of town plans in all countries would entail the use of existing plans. He therefore selected the best examples he could find and re-engraved them, acknowledging their authorship; for instance his plan of Haarlem (92) bears the inscription "dimensa a Pietro Wils Geometra 1646", and that of Enkhuisen "delineata a Cornelio Biens". He also used many maps from Braun and Hogenberg's atlas and hence, indirectly, those of Jacob van Deventer.

Blaeu's plans are expertly engraved and adorned with attractive vignettes. His presentation, however, lacks the consistency of van Deventer's in that the scale of plans was determined by the extent to which the subject would fit a double-folio page; the orientation is not uniformly with north at the top of the page; and neither the direction of north nor the scale of the plan are indicated. They have been summed up as "not a milestone in the history of cartography but a monument to the art of printing, engraving and bookbinding, a product of Amsterdam's culture at its greatest".[5]

REFERENCES

1. For much of the information in these pages, due acknowledgement is made to B. van 't Hoff, author of two articles, *De Nederlandsche gewestelijke Kaarten en stedeplattegronden vervaardigd door Jacobus van Deventer* and *Bijdrage tot de dateering van de oudere Nederlandsche stadsplattegronden*, published in Nederlandsche Archievenblad, 1939/40 and 1941/2 respectively.

2. British Museum Maps Library, reference c7d2.

3. POPHAM, A. E., *Georg Hofnagel and the Civitates Orbis Terrarum*, British Museum Maps Library.

4. Most of Blaeu's maps and plans of towns in the Netherlands are contained in the *Collection of Plans and Views of the United Provinces*, 24 volumes, edited by CRISTOFFEL BEUDEKER, 1728, British Museum Maps Library, reference c9d1.

5. FOCKEMA ANDREAE, S. J., *De Atlas van Blaeu*, Elsevier's Maandschrift, deel 84, 1932, p. 377.

General Bibliography

TOWN PLANNING, GENERAL

ABERCROMBIE, P., *Town and Country Planning*, 1943.

ADAMS, T., *Outline of Town and City Planning*, New York, 1935.

BERNOULLI, HANS, *Die Stadt und ihr Boden*, Zurich, 1946.

FOCKEMA ANDREAE, S. J., *Duizend Jaar Bouwen in Nederland*, Vol. I, Amsterdam, 1948.

GANSHOFF, F. L., *Etude sur le Développement des Villes entre Loire et Rhin au Moyen Age*, 1943.

KLOOS, W. B., *De Stedenbouwkundige Ontwikkeling in Nederland*, Amsterdam, 1947.

LAVEDAN, P., *Histoire de l'Urbanisme, Renaissance et Temps Modernes*, Paris, 1941.

MUMFORD, LEWIS, *Culture of Cities*, London, 1940.

PETERS, C. H. and BRUGMANS, H., *Oud-Nederlandsche Steden* (including *De Nederlandsche Stedenbouw*), 3 vols., Leiden, 1909.

SITTE, CAMILLO, *L'Art de Bâtir les Villes*, orig. Vienna, 1889.

TOUT, T. F., *Mediaeval Town Planning*, Manchester, 1934.

TOWNS, INDIVIDUAL

AMPSZING, S., *Beschrijving der Stad Haerlem*, 1728.

BREUNING, H. A., *Het Voormalige Batavia*, Amsterdam, 1954.

KOK, A. A., *De Historische Schoonheid van Amsterdam*, Amsterdam, 1941.

NIERMEYER, J. F., *Delft en Delfland*, Leiden, 1944.

STERCK-PROOT, J. M., *Historische Schoonheid van Haarlem*, Amsterdam, 1946.

VAN BEMMEL, A., *Beschrijving der Stad Amersfoort*, 1750.

VAN HASSELT, J. F. B., *Amersfoort rondom zijn Toren*, Amsterdam, 1948.

VAN OERLE, H., *Oud-Leiden*, Amsterdam, 1944.

WATTJES, J. G. and WARNERS, F. A., *Amsterdams Bouwkunst en Stadsschoon, 1306–1942*, Amsterdam, 1944.

WESTENDORP BOERMA, J. J., *De Historische Schoonheid van Zierikzee*, Amsterdam, 1946.

WORTEL, TH. P. H., *Oud-Alkmaar*, Amsterdam, 1943.

LAND RECLAMATION

COOLS, R. H. A., *Strijd om den Grond in het lage Nederland*, 's Gravenhage, 1949.

DIBBITS, H. A. M. C., *Nederland-Waterland*, Utrecht, 1950.

VAN VEEN, J., *Dredge, Drain, Reclaim*, The Hague, 1948, third edition, 1952.

HISTORY

BLOK, P. J., *History of the Dutch People*, Amsterdam, 1898–1912.

MOTLEY, J. L., *The Rise of the Dutch Republic*, London, 1871.

PIRENNE, H., *Mediaeval Cities*, 1923.

VLEKKE, B. H. M., *Evolution of the Dutch Nation*, New York, 1950.

WEDGWOOD, C. V., *William the Silent*, London, 1944.

MISCELLANEOUS

BEUDEKER, C., *Collection of Plans and Views of the United Provinces*, 1728.

BRAUN and HOGENBERG, *Civitates Orbis Terrarum*, 3 vols., Cologne, 1573–1617.

D'AILLY, A. E., *Catalogus van Amsterdamsche plattegronden*, 1938.

EAST, W. G., *An Historical Geography of Europe*, London, 1950.

EBERSTADT, R., *Neue Studien uber Stadtebau und Wohnungswesen*, Vol. II, 1914.

FERGUSSON, J., *History of Ancient and Mediaeval Architecture*, 1893.

GRASWINCKEL, D. P. M., *Nederlandsche Hofjes*, Amsterdam, 1944.

GUICCIARDINI, L., *Description of the Low Countreys . . .*, translated by G. Dannett, London, 1593.

HETTEMA, H., *Historische Schoolatlas*.

PLINY, *Naturalis Historia*, trans. H. Rackham, London, 1949–52.

SCHUKKING, W. H., *De Oude Vestingwerken van Nederland*, Amsterdam, 1948.

SITWELL, SACHEVERELL, *The Netherlands*, London, 1948.

SPEED, J., *Theatre of . . . Great Britain*, 1676.

TER KUILE, E. H., *Duizend Jaar Bouwen in Nederland (De Architectuur)*, Vol. I, Amsterdam, 1948.

'T HOOFT, P. J., *Dorpen in Zeeland*, Amsterdam, 1946.

VAN DEVENTER, JACOB, *Nederlandsche Steden in de 16ᵉ eeuw, Plattegronden*, No. 9, British Museum Maps Library.

VERHEIJEN, J., *Middeleeuwsche Nederlandsche Kloosters*, Amsterdam, 1947.

ARTICLES AND JOURNALS

FOCKEMA ANDREAE, S. J., *De Atlas van Bleau*, Elsevier's Maandschrift, deel 84, 1932.

MEARS, F., *The Planning of Mediaeval Cities*, Town Planning Institute Journal, Vol. X, No. 1.

POPHAM, A. E., *Georg Hofnagel and the Civitates Orbis Terrarum*, British Museum Maps Library.

VAN NIEROP, L., *De Huisen in het Noortsche Bosch*, 34st. Jaarboek van het Genootschaap AMSTELODAMUM, 1937.

VAN 'T HOFF, B., *De Nederlandsche gewestlijke Kaarten en stedeplattegronden vervardigd door Jacobus van Deventer and Bijdrage tot de dateering van de oudere Nederlandsche stadsplattegronden*, both published in the Nederlandsche Archievenblad, 1939/40 and 1941/2 respectively.

Glossary

bagijnhof	group of houses originally occupied by communities of R.C. women in Belgium, Holland and elsewhere who devoted them-selves to a religious life but retained the right of private property and were free to leave at any time; nowadays it houses old people.
bedstee or *bedstede*	bed placed in a square opening or recess behind the wall of a room.
boezem	system of reservoirs for superfluous polder water.
burcht	castle, citadel, stronghold.
dijk	dike, dyke, bank or embankment.
doel	target, butt.
doelen	enclosed space used, originally, as butts for training citizen armies in archery and later in the use of the arquebus and other firearms, and incorporating buildings for meetings, banquets, etc.
gasthuis	hospital, home for aged and infirm.
geestgrond	firm ground comprising a combination of clay, peat and archaic sand dunes; suitable for building development.
gracht(en)	canal(s) in a town, generally large enough to take barges.
grachtenstad	a town built upon low-lying or ill-drained land, necessitating extensive drainage work and the raising of the level of the land before building could take place.
hofje	almshouse in a close or courtyard founded and administered by a private trust.
keienstoepje	a *stoep* is a paved area in front of a house; a *keienstoepje* is a *stoep* paved in a mosaic pattern with pebbles.
meer	lake, loch or lough.
polder	artificially drained land, a diked marsh.
poort	gate, gateway.
proveniershuis	almshouse administered at public expense by a council appointed by the urban local authority.
secretarishuisje	a Town Clerk's official residence; no counterpart exists in Britain.
singel	moat of an outer wall, ramparts converted into promenade.

steeg   lane, alley.

stoof   footwarmer comprising wooden box with a grid of holes in the lid and containing a "test" or earthenware pot for charcoal.

terp   natural or man‑made hill or mound affording protection from seasonal floods.

vaart   waterway; *groote‑* for ocean‑going trade, *kleine‑* for home trade.

weg   way, road, path.

wijnhuis   wine house or wine shop.

Index

INDEX